T0137525

FOLIAGE

ADRIANA DARDAN

authorHOUSE®

AuthorHouse™
1663 Liberty Drive
Bloomington, IN 47403
www.authorhouse.com
Phone: 833-262-8899

Published by AuthorHouse   10/05/2020

ISBN: 978-1-6655-0308-2 (sc)
ISBN: 978-1-6655-0307-5 (e)

Print information available on the last page.

CONTENTS

To the lonely, the poor, and the abandoned, who built their secluded world from sufferings and painful memories, I dedicate this book, as a friend.

Adriana Dardan

FOREWORD

One of the most stimulating mental exercises is the study of human nature and behavior, which includes the ways of thinking, feeling, and actions that people tend to have naturally. It is a simple survey that does not require a special arrangement in an ornamental setting, or particular research to exclude what might be apparently insignificant. The personality of everyone can be deciphered in any circumstance that occurs spontaneously or deliberately.

Analyzing the details of human behavior confirms without a doubt that the nature of each individual is different from one to another, may be similar, or in rare cases, is unique. To postpone any detail and concentrate on the subject as a whole, will only miss many important features that can be obvious to the study.

One interesting aspects of the human nature is how people think about others. Personal or borrowed opinions are stretched on a large scale of the mental steadiness or emotional restlessness between the limits of falsehood and truth. In most cases, people tend to express negative opinions in particular about those who have proven success in their lives or have achieved goals that required effort, courage, and sacrifice. People learn a lot from each other. Filtering what is good from what is wrong in the human nature, builds a strong confidence in taking decisions and making the right choices. With little effort and only with willingness to observe the nature of people around, everyone's character can be sufficiently discerned and understood for shaping an accurate opinion. If not for other reason, perceiving and analyzing the development of the human ways of thinking, feeling, and acting, is the best way to know oneself.

Various sides of the human nature gathered through observation and personal experiences are described in this book.

Adriana Dardan

AUTUMN LEAVES

1. When you are young, love is everywhere around but you don't know what love is. It looks like a flame that lasts only as long as its brilliant light continues to shine for a short time and slowly fades away. Over the time, you discover its many ramifications, colorful aspects, and deceitful sites. When you are old, you know what love is, but you cannot find it any longer anywhere around. It is the unquenchable desire of a deep burning force that is more powerful than any other is, and only can reside in a disciplined mind. Knowing what love is when growing old is the work of wisdom, which shows a much richer chapter of emotions with fragrances like a light breeze unknown before. The autumn falling leaves around the tree are more colorful, the beauty of the morning has more radiance, and the peaceful evening

has more tranquility. Over a long time, you learned not only how to love people but also how to acquire the vision of loveliness they can express.

2.   The nature of people is like the autumn foliage. Everyone has something good, something bad, and something interesting to learn from. On top of the scale, are highly educated people, some of them with a very low standard of honesty, fairness, and compassion, but who are very resourceful in reaching big successes. On the bottom of the scale, are humble and uneducated people whose dearest wish is to give their kindness, consideration, and compassion to those in need. There are again, people in between, who take a more neutral, safe, and restricted pace of life by not expressing their true nature and by showing only what they consider to be without negative comments. Actually, there is no precise qualification of the human nature in this regard, and instead of analyzing details, which can be deceptive, everyone should be regarded as a particular character that has gradually developed over the course of life, and which has something different worth to be mentioned.

3. Temperament is a trait with which we are born and that can encourage many times the expression of anger. We are not born with anger and do not inherit it from our ancestors, but rather the aggressive attitude acquired throughout our lives could be considered as a reaction to discontent, to forcible compromises, and to abusive situations. Anger does not disappear as long as thoughts of resentment are fed by the idea that has determined them. Aggression is fueled by the desire to always be right and the inability to recognize with objectivity the position of the conflicting side. Anger is one of the most threatening forms of passion, and usually affects the one who manifests it, more than the one to which it is directed. In the complicated world in which we live, anger becomes inevitable and difficult to tolerate. It is different for everyone how to overcome the afflictions of the mind in terms of dispelling anger, and above all, it is different for everyone how to manage and to master an aggressive temperament that can only bring severe consequences.

4. Scientists and philosophers define the origin and evolution of life in many

phrases with big words, but don't tell what "life" is. Each has a different theory and explanation, depending on what they learned from the researchers before them, from personal experience, or just from exercising their own faith. Most of them agree that "life is the aspect of existence, and living itself defines life." Looking for a definition is actually not important except perhaps for linguists. What is important is how we live and how we face hardship and enjoy happiness, how well equipped we are to overcome difficulties, and how benevolent we are to share our experiences and kindly feelings with others. Some people say that life must have a purpose, or otherwise has no meaning. Some others ask themselves if life is worth the struggling for survival, but didn't find the answer. Most of the people just don't care and keep going. When asked what life is, an uneducated, homeless man said: "A walk toward tomorrow".

5.   People who work for living to support their families have no time to search for new theories and develop new systems of abstract thinking. The elite of the intellect is universally recognized to be

the prerogative of people with a vast capacity of knowledge and analytical power who became more scarce and less affirmed on the societal platforms. Those are the brilliant thinkers of humankind who mostly never had to work for living, most of them never had a family, and all of them had plenty of time to raise to a higher intellectual or spiritual level their thinking process based on deep knowledge and selective criteria. The beauty of their minds resides in their capacity of abstract thinking, but if any benefit in improvement of the human life doesn't follow, then the splendor of such an intellectual magnitude is worth only a performance or a work of art achieved as a custom for exercising the mental activity.

6.   If scientists would know what "thought" is, they would be able to implant it in a piece of wood, and make it think. They scanned the human brain to the thinnest slices, detected energies at different levels, but never could *read* the thought, which triggered them. They dissected the brain to the smallest bits, analyzed it to the level of atoms, without ever being able to find out what "thought" was. They only could

find how different parts of the brain are made, how they function, and how they work together, gave those parts fancy names, and described them in volumes of writings. However, they never could find how humans "think". Of course, reality as a particular position or point in space triggers our thoughts through information acquired by our senses from the simplest understanding, which then can evolve to the highest level of abstract connotation. How this information is processed at a frequency far greater than that of wavelength of light remains a total mystery in the scientific community for the time being, and most probably for all future time. Mind and brain are totally different. Reality is not always as easily perceived or understood, as it seems to be.

7. The feeling of contentment is usually active in most people and is expressed on a large scale from the smallest satisfaction to the fulfillment of the highest desires. People need to be satisfied, one way or another, and in most cases, contentment is based on their daily achievements or on their attainments extended over a long period. When the reason for contentment

is absent, the mind seeks an interlude and finds an incentive that triggers an illusion or a real fact capable of producing even an insignificant satisfaction. A breeze of fresh air, a flower that displays its colors in full sun, a bird that sits on the branch in front of the window, a dog that expresses its need for affection, are examples that produce small pleasures when someone is engaged in daily activities that do not allow postponement. Some people are satisfied with small pleasures that are available to anyone and which do not require explanation. Others neglect the small contents and seek satisfaction only in achieving special goals that can bring them recognition and fame. Some people are satisfied with the attention they receive from family, friends or even strangers. Others are pleased when they can provide warmth, love, help, and comfort to those around them. However, there are also enough people who have the feeling of content when they cause suffering, pain, and commit crime. This category includes those who cannot fit into the normal rhythm of a daily existence. Full and permanent contentment is only acquired by those people who know and respect the human values and who live in accordance with a code of ethics based on a moral excellence.

8. Poverty is not a disease, and yet it has become a worldwide pandemic. Also, poverty is not a crime, but an injustice and a great mistake for which no one apologizes. Poverty is the result of inequality and the way in which an organized society declines any obligation towards those who fail to make a contribution to the common prosperity. The causes are multiple and the consequences are similar to those who become poor for health reasons, family reasons, societal reasons, or reasons of physical and mental tension caused by fear of a dark future. When poverty becomes a source of irritation for society, people fallen into poverty begin to be invisible, neglected, and outcast. They are lying on the streets, in parks, under bridges and in places where they cannot be seen. They clothe with rags, eat garbage, are totally lacking in hygiene and medical care. They take refuge in an isolated world where most of them live from painful memories that no one knows. They are lonely people without family, without friends, living

abandoned in a deserted world in which each one passes in the shadow of the other in a creepy atmosphere where from time to time only sounds of sighing are heard. Malnutrition, cold, and diseases gradually exterminate them, and other poor, lonely, and abandoned take their places.

9. The value of a house is estimated by the competitors' prices on the market. So is a piece of jewelry, and so is every single outer value in the world. How about the inner values? How do we estimate them? We do not. Love, kindness, generosity, are part of the human nature. We are usually tempted to achieve goals with values that are demanded by others, and we are forgetting to bring our own values to the same platform. Sometimes it is easier to fabricate values that only feel real, than to offer those that already exist and which are real but personal. It is a natural tendency to cover what we do not want to be known by those around us, either from modesty or from the uncertainty that we have in the solidity of our character. However, let's not forget that the values we offer on the societal platform are part of the culture, civilization and way of

life in collaboration with those around us. If we can bring our contribution, no matter how small, we should be proud of ourselves.

10. It is said that old age is not only ugly, but even very ugly. The assertion depends on the subjectivity of the assessor. Knowing how to get older is a form of wisdom and a difficult chapter in knowing how to live. Old age is the time to understand the hidden details of life, it is the time to affirm the past good and bad experiences, and it is the precious time to analyze with objectivity the achievements as well as the mistakes that have constituted the column of support for all decisions, confrontations, and successes. The teachings of the books are set aside, and replaced with the teachings of the existent realities. Old age is not the time of silence, but the valuable time of sharing a precious wisdom gathered over the years, with those who come after and have the desire to accept it. It could be said in good faith that old age, if it's not beautiful, certainly is not ugly.

11. Whoever affirms that is fearless makes a completely untrue statement. In

every human being and in every other creature fear is permanently rooted as an instinctive trait that cannot be altered and which is designed as part of survival. At the beginning of the emergence of the human species, noise and falling were the first reactions to fear that developed into instincts of survival and were transmitted to the generations who followed. Over time fear has accumulated complex aspects, following the human development, and became associated with countless emotional reactions that were modulated by knowledge and learning. From the simple reaction of a survival instinct, fear has become a rational process that can be analyzed and accepted as such, or an agglomeration of irrational feelings explained only by a process overextended beyond reasonable limits. Fear of the unknown is common and prevalent to all people who live constantly with uncertainty about their daily existence. Fear of death is petrifying and more than the other aspects of fear, it has the power to completely inhibit the rational ways of thinking. We wonder, how we can deal with the many aspects of fear that are constantly around us? There is no acceptable answer. Everyone is more or less equipped to minimize the effects of fear and exercise control over it but no one cane eradicate it, not even for a moment. Since there is no award for being afraid, at the bottom line we should compromise and assert that perhaps fear makes us appreciate and protect more the values of life.

12. As time goes by, it leaves behind only very few dear moments to be remembered and cherished. People who find in each other, features of themselves that are reflected back to them with amplitude and start expanding with greatness, share those moments. People who show similarities in their thoughts and feelings look always to broaden their ways of communicating with more understanding, meaning that the range of what each feels and thinks warrants a big amplification never to be doubted. On the other hand, each one has feelings and thoughts that are not similar, but meet on a platform of challenges that makes them desirable to be accepted and adopted by both sides. If they are, those features are cognitively intensified and expand in the pattern of behavioral characteristics of each individual.

13. Everyone likes company and a pleasant conversation, which is ideal when, becomes a sharing of thoughts and feelings. When you face someone who talks a lot of nonsense and rambles with no particular interesting subjects, keep silent, and try listening. That someone will always try to show knowing better than you any subject heard and repeated from other people. When you face someone who is more educated and talks about topics hard for you to understand, keep silent and try listening. That someone will try to impress you with an eloquent exhibition of wit and with the profundity of the subject. When you face someone of your class, your talking is well received and the conversation becomes an intelligent dialog of listening to what is said and to answer to the purpose. It becomes a delightful gratification, and is highly valued by both sides.

14. Family is the nucleus of heredity. The offspring is nurtured with care, love, and teachings to survive and grow up. Slowly the child learns skills, familiar features, and in the framework of values, he understands how to accept what is good and reject what is harmful. The first and

most important premise to be grasped by those who want to form a family and to become parents is that the greatest part of their time should be given to the effort and care of raising their child. The family should always provide a secure climate in which a child can feel free to develop his mind, never to be scared to share his problems, always be able to count on the support of his parents. A child should always look up to his parents if they prove a strong relationship, showing love and respect to each other and build with care a warm climate for all the members of the family. If parents behave angrily, abusive, or threateningly to each other, the child becomes scared, hides his feelings, adopts his parents attitude as a reaction to protect himself, becomes noncompliant, and reveals signs of depression and social alienation. The disheartened child grows up and becomes an angry adult who lacks confidence, self-esteem, and willpower to be integrated in the continuous stream of the societal development.

15. One of the most distressing states of mind is the continuous circling of stray thoughts, without any contingence among them, keeping the same rhythm, moving

constantly without aim, and trying in vain to reach a meaningful purpose. The human mind is never content with peace, and if deprived of activity, its faculties become tired, its strength is diminished, and everything around seems sinking. With small or great effort, a goal appears on the horizon, and the thought which determines it becomes predominant. The mind starts believing what eventually becomes a potential aspect for action. Taking the first step, the mind will mobilize its dynamics and will show the way toward action, which is a great restorer and a reliable builder. Once a plan for a new exploration is designed, the entire thinking process is channeled toward a meaningful accomplishment to bring a sense of being alive and proud.

16. The adversities of life are encountered at every step we take, no matter how much we want to anticipate a quiet and free from hindrances way. On the other hand, if there were no difficulties, the evolution of humankind would have been a continuous state of languishing, and without the heights of progress that were necessary for both, individual and societal development. Life is deeply

understood by those who have overcome hardship and have encountered its adversities through efforts and sacrifices. Those who have received all the benefits without making any effort, and consider life as a privilege given to them, sooner or later fall apart, become selfish, insensible, and totally alien to life's real values. The experiences we go through, teach us to value what we do through effort, mistakes, and laborious activity, but especially teach us to extract the moments of wisdom we learned and which help us to go forward.

17. We come into this world bringing with us a package filled with inherent attributes: health, strength, feelings, capacity for reasoning. From the beginning, we are aware of close people called "family" who surround us with warmth, care, and devotion. We begin to develop our senses and our personality, and we start understanding something of what is called "life". We meet strangers who are kind to us and we call them "friends", and others who are aversive to us and we call them "enemies". On the many paths in front of us, we learn how to choose what is right and how to define an acceptable

social behavior. We learn and know the inherited values that we begin to cherish, and we add to them the new ones that we construct with the ability of the mind and the complexity of the soul. We are constantly learning from both positive and negative experiences, we work hard to provide the necessary support for the family and to develop perspectives that will become the basis for the formation of future generations. On the long journey of our life, we have achieved useful goals, we made countless mistakes, and we have reached the point where the conclusion of our merit exposes itself, giving us the sense of success or failure. From there on, faith takes over reason, since we don't know if there is anything further. To the package we came with, we added our personal contribution: love, generosity, compassion, a code of ethics, devotion and sacrifices, which we can share with those whom eventually we will encounter in an unknown world waiting for us.

18. Giving advice is like tossing a two sides coin: win or lose. Most of the people who ask for advice, know the answer to their problem, but they hope to find a different

one. If the person who is asked for advice is someone famous, or highly intellectual, or very knowledgeable in Greek history, the given advice is taken without any doubts that might be the wrong one. Coming from a modest and uncultivated mind, the advice could be the right one, but will never be considered. It is in the nature of people to have high regard for those who acquired a reputation of being "smart" and their thinking is never questionable. It so happened many times, that someone with a modest background is more capable to take a right decision, make a more reasonable choice, and find the best solution to the problem by giving the best advice that could solve an intricate situation. Just because that someone relies only on the humble resort called "common sense".

19. Nobody can live free from attachment and aversion alike, without being overwhelmed by the confusions of good and evil when these two sides of demeanor come too close to each other. Being able to choose between the two of them requires presumption of knowing the outcome. Everyone needs wisdom but not everyone has it.

Wisdom and understanding are slowly built through experience, observation, and perseverance, and only after, they can be applied to judgment and search in finding the truth. Through discernment, comprehension, and perspective, we can find out the limitations of our possibilities which are reflected in our strength to choose between good and evil. In our complicated world, for the time being, we only can realize how little we can understand about life, about people, about ourselves, and most of all, about the great mystery into which we were born.

20. There is much beauty in this world, and there is much ugliness. Try to see and understand both sides and judge everything with fairness. Try to reach the human mind where knowledge resides and no matter how much you know, there is always someone above you, and someone below. Try to reach the mind and soul of that one who is above you. Try to learn as much as you can, because knowledge broaden your horizon and is the most delightful and rewarding inner bliss a human being can have. From books we learn how minds and feelings were

triggered by factors of evolution in search for new meanings of life, and for better understanding among people of different cultures. From exchanging information between people, we learn the skill of communication, which makes us close to each other. From experiencing the world with our senses, we learn how nature was created and how to share among us with mutual understanding a place called "Earth". From everything, from everyone, and from ourselves, the more we learn the more is left to be learned.

21. I spotted a housefly walking up and down my patio window. It is one of the most disgusting creatures, it lives on decaying material, it is filthy, carries pathogens but doesn't die of them, sucks blood, and is very annoying. Certainly, scientists found for it a precise place in the process of evolution, and probably a good reason for it to exist. Well, since I am not a scientist, I am allowed to say that it is distasteful and worthless. Looking at it under a magnifier, it looks like a monster, and yet, the parts of its body are of an amazing design, starting with its compound eyes, and continuing with its translucent wings, which in less

than thirty milliseconds can detect a threat and change the course of its flight. It might be a beauty for entomologists, but for me the housefly will always be a repulsive and filthy pest. The world would be a better place to live without it. At least, my patio would be. Why am I writing this? Because I just got annoyed, thinking that such a distasteful creature can be of such a marvelous design.

22. Over the course of millions of years, the human race has managed to advance and lead the other species with which it traversed the historical time of the process of evolution. The thinking capacity that human has acquired has become the supreme power that gives him the dominant superiority over all biological organisms. Humanity is the result of lengthy processes of struggle, antagonism, cruelty, destruction, and constraint of human dominance by human. Nevertheless, from these series of actions, in the midst of cruelty and tragedy it was possible to achieve societal and individual developments at the levels of thinking that formed civilizations and cultures on a basis of collaboration and understanding. The gap between the

highest and the lowest place in society is huge in today's world, and is imperative to decrease at the most, and on the whole should become free from disturbance. Undoubtedly, the humankind can reach and maintain its glory only through moral integrity, friendship among nations, education, and intellect development.

23. One way or another everyone worries about something that occurs, or might occur. Rich people worry about investments that are meant to bring them more money and to enhance their wealth. Scientists worry about new theories for which they don't know the truth, but have to be published in any case, just to keep them on the competition floor. Highly intellectual people worry about their reasoning pursuits that with every passing day have a lesser demand in the advancement of knowledge. Working people worry about their insecure jobs that can be ended at any time and leaving their family without support. Poor people have no worries, because there is nothing left in their lives to be worried about. However, since they have a lot of free time, they choose to worry about the world, which is speeding up on a fast

track, rapidly deteriorating, trashing all the inherited values, and leaving behind only damages, diseases, and degradation, for the next generation, which certainly will have plenty to worry about.

24. Our body is made of tiny miracles called "cells". They are by the trillions and live in groups in different areas, depending on their skill and trade. Their home is spotless clean and awesomely decorated with complex patterns. In the middle is located the main room called "nucleus" where life resides. Around are tiny appliances, bearing names given by scientists, hard to pronounce and even harder to remember. Each one of those has a job to perform with the precision of a sub-atomic clock. The trillions of cells live in a perfect harmony, helping each other and taking care of each other. Had they had a mind of their own, our body would have become a pack of rags-and-tatters right after birth. Well, perhaps a little later, they would have learned how to kill each other without having any regrets, just as people do.

25. Searching for the truth is a strenuous process that requires a careful positioning

of each piece of the assembly at the exact place where it fits. At one point, however, the parts are depleted and the projected assembly remains unfinished, bearing only a shadow of hope in finding the truth. Then comes in the presumption that anticipates the probability of a fictitious result, considered as a conclusion of the researched goal. The parts that may fit together must connect to each other and have a logic-like communication similar to the nerve cells network, which denotes the evidence of a purpose-oriented, error-free function. Presumption is a process in which the arrangement of the necessary parts starts from a hypothetical reasoning in search for the truth. The conclusion remains in the most frequent cases built from ideas taken to be true, while the search for answers remains open. Sometimes though, the logic of reasoning becomes victorious and the truth appears concluding, even if it is discovered on theoretical basis rather than through real considerations.

26. Man and woman are born predators. They steal, fight, kill, and are rapacious. They inherited the feature of predation from their very old ancestors, the first

humans who lived two millions years ago, and used it only as a means of survival. With the passing of time, hatred, envy, animosity, enmity, revenge, and many features alike, were added to the nature of humans, making them a wide-ranging predator species, much above all the others. Societal laws and religion stepped in with special purpose to assuage the escalating use of predation and to minimize its extension in becoming an epidemic. Nevertheless, the inherited feature proved to be more powerful than the paragraphs of laws and the religious scripts. Over the past centuries, people became fanatic, ferocious, and without trace of being humans, by inventing physical and mental tortures, mutilations, mass killings, and genocides. For as long as genetics is active and the inherited, dreadful gene will not be silenced, the chance for eradicating the feature of predation in humans is close to none.

27. A child is born in time of the war. Before he sees the loving smile of his mother, he notices the tears of suffering that run down her cheeks. Before he can hear the soft music of a lullaby, he perceives the thunderous sound of bombs and

machine-gun bursts. Before he can enjoy the beneficial light of the sun, he notices the opaque darkness of the camouflage and the flame of a candle that goes out. Before he learned the simple talk of games and joys, he mastered the complicated language of adversity and the bitter fighting spoken by the adults. Much long before time, the child comes into the world of the grown-ups and long before he knows what a toy is, he finds out what a fighting weapon is and how it is used. When the war is over the young generation who never knew what love, forgiveness, and consideration for the human life is, becomes the bearer of the torch of hatred, revenge, and murder.

28. Ambitious people race in the competition for fame and name recognition on the societal platform, using all the means available to them, regardless if an ethical engagement is taken into consideration or fraudulent intentions that could lead to aggravation for others are decided as a better choice. The rivalry between two or more people becomes bitter and fierce on the way to success and the advantage is on the side of the one who proved to be a more powerful fighter. However,

the success, which was achieved, is not long lasting if it is not sustained by the objective that initiated it. When for example, the initial goal is considered a scientific discovery of world value, the name and fame of the one who won the competition remain in history. Nevertheless, usually, the pursuit for glory and fame gets tired, the supporting resources diminish, and the name of the winner in the competition disappears in time and remains forgotten.

29. Over the long period of time since their emergence, humans have learned to adapt themselves to climate changes, nutrition variation, reconsideration of vital needs, all factors that led to the physical and mental ability to adjust to more suitable conditions of existence. The natural changes forced the human adaptability to comply with the environment and became a condition for survival. The accumulation of changes became beneficial when the organism succeeded in overcoming the hardship that came along and complied with the entire dynamic process of accumulating favorable changes without proving new vulnerabilities. Changes occur daily

and affect to a certain extent, the body, mind, behavior, and constitution of the character. How everyone reacts to these changes and how these changes are accepted depend on the needs, the circumstances in which they occur, the interconnection of social relations, and most of all, on the perspective of improving the conditions of life. After a very long time, the adaptability to man-made changes prevailed over to the natural ones.

30. Almost all creatures on Earth use sounds and gestures to communicate within the same group that presents similar characteristics of one member with others. In the first periods of its appearance, resembling to the other creatures, the way of communication of humans consisted exclusively of sounds and gestures that expressed uncomplicated needs and feelings. Over the long passing of time, amplified sounds could be articulated into simple words with special meaning and precise definition. The words became complex, forming phrases, and further establishing the basic of an everyday language. The spoken way between the groups of humans was

neither understood nor assimilated in common except in cases where different kind of groups were forced by natural conditions or by hostile conflicts to live together. From those combinations of different human assemblages, new languages have emerged and developed throughout the millennial history. Each language represents in a unique way the culture of a nation expressed in speech and writing, and which is integrated into the worldwide treasure of humanity. If all the other creatures could use words, people could learn a lot from them, become wiser, gentler, more generous and compassionate, and the world would be a much better place to live.

31. Sincerity is a fragile trait of character and often proves to be insufficiently equipped to meet the resistance motivated by doubt and mistrust. At the very young age of childhood, thoughts and feelings are not filtered through the canvas of experience and discernment, and sincerity is usually considered naive. With the passage of time, the call to hypocrisy appears as a welcome solution when sincerity cannot be pursued without the risk of becoming offensive or causing doubt in motivating

the truth. Sincere people are known to be respected for their honesty and are highly appreciated for the confidence that can inspire others, especially when acute problems need to be resolved. However, when sincerity is masked by the coat of hypocrisy in order to gain one's trust by displaying false claims, the pursued interests even if sometimes prove to be fruitful, the satisfaction obtained is lesser than the degradation of the character that bears the seal of contempt forever. Especially, the time that follows proves a state of self-loathing and a deep feeling of being unworthy of one's consideration.

32. In this complicated world in which the essential attribute of life has become a struggle for success, the pressure that permanently acts on both, physical body and mind, transforms the normal nature of people into a continuous strain for affirmation. The feeling of physical or emotional tension comes from any event or thought that causes dissatisfaction, anger, or nervousness, and usually starts in the family. The children express their wishes that cannot be fulfilled, the spouse has displeasure at work from the boss who is not satisfied with the level

of the work done, the mother-in-law is unhappy with the way she is treated, and so on. At the workplace, everyone brings many personal problems, discusses them, amplifies them, adds them to the pressure exerted by the deadlines of the works, and the tension instead of decreasing, jumps up. On the way back home, the traffic is intense, people are nervous, they get angry, and sometimes they become aggressive. Because there is no escape from this kind of stressful life, from time to time everyone needs to go away and spend some time in solitude. The peace and silence of the nature, helps the organism and the mind to restore their normal functions, while new strength gives the feeling of life itself being regained. Since there is no other way to establish a permanent balance between intense activity and fatigue, searching for solitude from time to time seems to be the best formula to find oneself on the right path.

33. Silence and sound are inversely related and act by turns without interfering with each other when coming from the same source. Together they are found in nature, in the life of every creature, in the

human life, and both are necessary to the same extent in the course of existence. When the sound increases in intensity to the maximum level, the silence gradually decreases to the full extent. In psychology, sound and silence are defined as two separate notions that have a mutual effect and that together form an integral whole. It seems to be the exact translation of what we know from reality. Both are necessary and useful as long as they act in balance with the acceptance of the organism and continue to be beneficial to health. A continuous noisy environment becomes harmful to both the organism and the way of thinking, compared to the harmonious sound of the music or the pleasing auditory expressions of nature that bring an atmosphere of calm and relaxation. On the other hand, complete long-term silence is no less harmful, because the brain deprived of sounds for a longer time, becomes refractory to stillness, and generates an activity in this direction, which results in ringing, buzzing, and humming. It is up to everyone to find the right pathway for the most suitable level of sound and silence and make it acceptable.

34. Many times the mind shows signs of fatigue without a special cause. Perhaps it is because of the daily many problems that cannot be solved, or perhaps because of many encountered dissatisfactions, or perhaps the overwork forces its activity to unfold at an uncontrollable pace. In spite of everything, people are not satisfied with peace of mind for a longer period. They need activity and if they don't find it around them, they build it from prospects that can provide a wide field of action, which even if it is not planned as an initial goal, it focuses on necessary improvements for an optimal implementation of an existing project. The human mind is permanently active. During sleep and dreams, the brain works continuously to eliminate the energies consumed during the day, and the regeneration of the mind is prepared for the thinking process that follows, and is necessary in the performances that emerge and require it. A short break from time to time is welcome for the relief of mental fatigue when thoughts seem to be heavy and unable to function under a normal and unimpeded development. A glimpse at the beauty of the nature for a few instants, an exchange of amicable

words with the neighbor, a kind gesture granted to a friend, there are moments when the brain relaxes and the thought recovers its normal rhythm.

35. We always talk and hear about conscience as a specific human characteristic discovered since the time of the first manifestations of the abstract thinking. Science defines conscience as a cognitive process that causes rational associations based on a system of individual values. Philosophy defines conscience as a complex of moral principles that dictate individual actions. It is well known though that human behavior does not conform to definitions, but rather to the realities encountered daily, step by step. In simplistic expression, conscience is the trait considered of the highest individual value, since it cannot be shared. It is the inner view of the human mind that analyzes and measures with the greatest accuracy the thought and the effect of its consequences. It is the mentor and the intimate consultant who reveals with certainty the repercussions of the actions initiated and of those of the actions taken. It is a law and a judge at the same time, and does not admit compromises in the

objective application of justice. Each one of us makes mistakes superficial or serious, but we can never forgive ourselves even if we are forgiven by others. Conscience never fails rightness.

36. We detect the state of things as they actually exist through our biological senses the same as all the other existing creatures, then we apply our perception that represents the interpretation, selection and organization of all the sensorial information. Reality is outright while perception is relative and is based on the way in which everything around us determines our personal interpretation based on understanding or intuitive recognition. Perception also encompasses the circumstances in which everyone responds to the accumulated information. It is a process in which we receive sensorial information from the external environment and use them for interconnection with the particular conditions in which we live. The senses that are triggered react in the mode in which the received information are processed by the cerebral nervous system, and determine in continuation the corresponding action. Unlike other

creatures, humans have the natural ability to possess feelings caused by brain processes which are independent of the activity of sensorial information. People can become happy, sad, angry, they can feel fear, shame, guilt, and they can feel strong emotions only by relying on past experiences which are reactivated through memory. Also, people can seek refuge in imagination and build a fake reality from desires, intentions, relationships, and so on. Emerged either from sensorial information, or from past experiences, or from imagination, feelings affect the human body by a physiological change that concludes in a behavioral response.

37. It is proper to the human nature to build a safe, comfortable existence, with all that is necessary for a carefree life. It is also in the human nature to want to have more than is necessary and to acquire material goods that provide people with wealth, luxury, extravagance, and livelihoods corresponding to a system of life well above a balanced level. The human society, at first simple and unpretentious, has become throughout the historical times, more and more

complex and difficult, demanding from people more and more effort to fulfill all the obligations that required harder work and broader qualification. Each economic sector opens the way for a similar one that is not really necessary, but represents only a lot of increased possibilities for investments and material profits. It seems then that the human society becomes prosperous and people have a rich existence in which the limits are no longer measurable by the physical and mental power of the population but only by the extent of economic fluctuations. People's lives have become so complicated that simplicity is no longer able to extract the essence that organizes what appears complex and confusing. We cannot go back to simplicity to eliminate what is useless and harmful, but we must not even consider simplicity as stagnation, boredom, or lack of new perspectives. We can eliminate and clean up many useless aspects of the existence by expanding the space around us, being convinced that having more and wanting to have more is a road that ends up with a slow death. Simplifying our existence by focusing on what is necessary, we can breathe easier, find joy at every step, appreciate the beauties of life, and understand better the human values.

38. Life has multiple sites with different landscapes, which display shapes, and colors that change with every attempt to approach them. If you start the journey by walking slowly, every field of questionable perception encountered at each step, will be uncovered with confidence, and will disclose the meanings you are looking for. You learn, you teach, you understand, and you acquire what your mind needs to develop into a world of thoughts and feelings that can open a higher level of reason and intellectual knowledge. You discover new perspectives with wider views, which enlarge the rich environment of cognizance, and build new bridges of communication with your peers. On the path of your long journey, you will ascertain that what is worth living is above self-contentment. If you can find it, you are alive.

39. During distinct historical periods, highly intelligent people made substantial contributions to the development of abstract and experimental thinking. History does not mention whether those

brilliant people were proud of their achievements or considered their efforts as merely a necessity of work as a reason for their purpose. There is no mention either if they were just satisfied with the results of their work, which during their lifetime was little or not acknowledged. Pride is a secondary trait of the human character and is insignificant as long as it does not underline the unobserved importance of a valuable work or the unseen efforts of the one who did it. Self-respect is necessary and admirable as long as a person properly assesses one's qualities and defects, and does not pass the acceptable limit of pride, when one comes close to the position of a false self-appreciation. Someone who uses pride to boast of being humble is actually found to be hypocritical and usually succeeds through a visibly insincere attitude to attract the admiration from others. Also, excessive self-pride becomes arrogant and defiant. Dignity is a preferable trait, which unlike pride, is significant and becomes stable in any situation where it can be observed and is considered a quality of character.

40. Throughout our lives we learn to distinguish the qualities and flaws of people according to the code of ethics that we have established as a standard for our personal behavior. We are drawn to and approach people who denote qualities similar to ours and we move away from those whose flaws we consider offensive. Moreover, we have the sentimentality of admiration, for someone who denotes values and qualities that we do not have but that we would like to have. Sometimes people experience envy and ill will when qualities encountered in others cause them feelings of inferiority. It is the prerogative of everybody to accept or not oneself as well as the others whenever they are put face to face. We admire the moral beauty emanating from a balanced thinking system that reveals generosity, compassion, altruism, and kindness. From the people we admire we can learn traits emanating from their ability to accumulate through selection, accuracy, and tenacity, the faculty to successfully perform physical and mental efforts. The feeling of admiration expressed for worthy people is just as exhilarating as that expressed for artistic and cultural

values, and their combination brings to existence a unique sense of gratification.

41. We inherit some genes from parents and perhaps some from ancestors, which together will establish to an adequate degree the foundation of our character formation. From the earliest childhood, the characteristics of our behavior are influenced by the environment of family, friends, and even strangers. Character traits begin to distinguish and outline the beginnings of stabilizing our moral values that gradually define our personality and behavioral principles based on discernment. Over time, knowledge and understanding of the fragments of existence collaborate in the construction of the human character, piece by piece, not leaving any gaps between them. The character gradually stabilizes and outlines the ethics and the virtues in which one believes and on which all decisions are based, through analyzing and choosing the factors that affect the logical reasoning. Character traits are of great significance in successfully achieving a desired purpose, in relationships with people and in the way that one is accepted by the society.

An admirable character is regarded to have among other moral virtues, honesty, responsibility, compassion, generosity, and consideration for people's needs. Being honest and keeping your honor whole is vital in believing in yourself, is essential in your relationships with others and is indispensable for everything you want to achieve in life.

42. People are companionable beings, living together, and sharing duties, needs, successes, and failures. Family rules establish collaborative and supportive relationships between its members who know their obligations as well as their merits, and who contribute to the common prosperity. The societal rules define the necessary and accepted behavior in the common organization in which people share an economic, cultural and industrial superstructure. Nevertheless, it is often the case that events or people inspire feelings of adversity that affect the well-being of a family member or of a social group. In these occurrences, people react differently, some withdraw into apathy, others react with hostility, and others become disoriented and reject a normal behavior by adopting a bizarre

attitude. In many instances, people feel alienation, detected as disharmony with their true self. Also, the rapid changes in the society, as well as the traditional values that are challenged, determine the impossibility for some people to keep their ideals in which they believe. This experience calls for finding a place that still remains unaltered and is open only for isolation. In these cases, people affected by alienations, withdraw from a normal existence, some descend into total inactivity, while others build their own ideology in which they promote violence and revenge.

43. It is said that seeing is believing and perhaps it is so. However, we must mention that appearances can deceive us. We believe what we see only in cases where our observations refer to immovable subjects whose shape, color, size and position are not in doubt. As for people, their outer look is beyond doubt, and what we see is undoubtedly to be believed. However, their attitude, gestures, speech, are momentary aspects that change from one situation to another and indicate apparent doubts in the transitory reality, as well as doubts

in the probability of being repeated. Accepting without a doubt what people are talking, means to accept their statements as being true, only if those statements are justified to be considered without question. People's opinions are expressed by their character and in most cases reveal a degree of inconsistency between the conveyed thinking and the behavior that actually exists. The distrust of what people say or do usually occurs when people in question have repeatedly demonstrated instability in similar statements or actions. We are inclined to trust family members, or valuable friends, or strangers with a reputation for honesty and moral principles. We learn through experience to recognize doubt in what seems to be true, and we learn to distinguish the altered way in which people try to present the truth. In simplistic terms, everything that exists in life is doubtful, but everything becomes difficult in the absence of trust between people and especially in the lack of self-trust. To see, to think, and to feel with complete confidence, without doubt, is contrary to the human character.

44. Opinion is like a ball thrown from one person to another, sometimes it is caught, and sometimes it falls to the ground. Opinion is a point of view or an appreciation exercised by the mind without necessarily considering the expression of the evidence. Usually an opinion is determined by perspectives, feelings, desires, or impressions that are produced by an eventual fulfillment of a purpose. People with different opinions can argue the opposite, even if they agree with the facts that led to the arguments. An opinion becomes justifiable when it is supported by concrete facts and is recognized as reasonable. People who seek the opinion of others on personal issues, either need help in solving a difficult situation, or want to receive assurance in the decision they have made and are waiting for confirmation from others. Usually the opinions given by people contain a dose of subjectivism that comes from the desire to become useful or from pride when it comes from the desire to be recognized as skilled and understanding persons. Opinions coming from the community usually contain prejudices that influence the individual and sometimes prevent him

from expressing his personal views that may be different. Likewise, opinions revealed by passions do not usually have support, and are only a sign of affectation shown by people lacking any conviction and who covet only for self-approval.

45. Humans are sociable creatures. They need each other's company; they live together, talk, laugh, cry, share thoughts and feelings, and depend on each other. We are always inclined to share with our family and friends the feelings of joy, our successes, and our prospects we want to achieve. We can easily express what we think and feel when those we address have a friendly attitude and a desire to understand and know our personality. Nevertheless, we manage to transpose our thoughts and feelings into a false expression when we observe that people we talk to, display misleading intentions caused by lack of honesty. The only feeling we cannot mask and falsify is sadness. We are never sufficiently prepared to reveal to others what causes the painful emotion of sadness we feel and about which we do not wish to comment on. In this case, we adopt the refuge in a temporary isolation, which becomes the

only mechanism of protection and relief by which we try to accept the reason that has generated our moral weakness culminated in depression. We analyze the cause and try to accept the reality. With the passage of time, sadness turns into a feeling of melancholy with which we are obliged to get used to and which we accept as a refuge to be always there for us, whenever we need it.

46. Your friend is severely depressed, lost hopes and courage, sees no way out, and asks nothing from you but to be left alone. Well, this is a crucial moment when your friend needs your help, your understanding, and compassion. Most of all, what your friend needs, is not to be left alone. There are moments when friendship and fidelity show the strong bond of most people's deepest emotional well-being, and in those moments, a true friend should stand up for the other one, without any reserve. Never expect to be praised for your abilities and for your good will that you struggled hard to show. If you feel that your intentions to help are worth the friendship you honored, then you should be content,

since you showed a great care for your friend just for being there.

47. People find inspiration in everything and in everyone where they can observe attributes that reflect characteristics similar to theirs, or traits that determine a desire to initiate perspectives with new meanings. Anyone and anything alive or dead, real or imaginary can become a source of inspiration. The human mind is always more active than usually when new stimuli trigger new thoughts, new feelings, new reactions. Inspiration stimulates people who are going through a period of apathy and want to try a new standpoint of possibilities. A piece of landscape with colorful flowers and hills on the far site inspires a peaceful feeling of being away for a while from a turbulent world. A monarch butterfly displaying its marvelous design inspires the long time languid desire for painting again and to unveil the aptitude in which no one believed. Human beings need each other and especially they need behavioral examples that influence the faculty to think positively and to select a fair decision from the available options. People are influenced not only by those

who have been recognized in history for their exceptional achievements, but also by ordinary ones who prove a firm standard of moral values in their daily attitude. Someone who expresses generosity, warmth, kindness and understanding for others, inspires admiration and the desire to be imitated. Nevertheless, someone who is a menace, who is abusive, who has a negative way of living, can easily become an inspirational source of maleficent behavior for emotionally distraught people. Inspiration is a choice and not a duty or commitment.

48. The word "sacrifice" has two different meanings. Although considered as virtue, sacrifice is not an essential trait in the sense of moral values that motivates the attitude and guides the achievement of the purpose. Some people sacrifice time, money, and energy, relationships, even family, for the successful fulfillment of a purpose that will reward them with moral and material benefits. In this sense, sacrifice becomes a means of giving a series of values only to acquire something more valuable in the future. Other people who denote a strong moral character make sacrifices in favor of others, either

for family, friends, neighbors, or for the community in which they live. In this category belong those who do not expect a reward for what they give, but are pleased that they have the opportunity to help and improve the existence of those around them. Although everyone has the opportunity to make sacrifices in favor of others, there are not many who are strong enough to give partially or totally to others what is essential to their personal existence. Those who sacrifice for others whom they do not even know, or for the achievement of a valuable purpose, are considered to have the highest level of virtue. Helping those in need is sometimes an act of great sacrifice, but the satisfaction of succeeding in improving one's existence is incomparable to any other satisfaction that one can have. Sacrifice is not always virtuous; sometimes people sacrifice themselves for an unjust cause and in these cases their sacrifice is transposed into an action that becomes harmful and useless.

49. We make mistakes every day, our entire life. Some are small, some are big, some can be forgiven, and others are

unforgettable. There is no one exempt from making mistakes, since we cannot control ourselves at every step and we cannot always be sure that the decision we have made is the right one. We are forced to deal with mistakes and accept what cannot be changed anymore. We must learn the realities of life as they are and not as we would like them to be. The feeling of mistakes we've made follows us continuously in life, and gives us a permanent state of helplessness which translates into accepting our guilt that cannot be obliterated. We have made mistakes towards people and many of them have forgiven us, but their benevolent attitude is not enough to eliminate the guilt we have and can never be erased. As long as we cannot forgive ourselves, we cannot forget and forgive the mistakes we have made. The memory of all the wrong we did is accompanied by grief over the inability we proved when we made the incorrect decisions that led to unwanted results, and left behind the feeling of regret. We would like the feeling of antagonism we have against our conscience in this direction to be a sufficient punishment for our regrets and to be able to eradicate the memory of our mistakes. This power is not in the human structure since the mind will never give up the feeling of guilt.

50. There is no one so well known to others as to be exempt from becoming a subject of either benevolent or hostile prejudice. A preconceived idea that is not based on reason or experience becomes an uncertain consideration regarding religion, nationality, race, or mere attitude that is different from what is common. It would be fair for people not to draw conclusions based on manufactured opinions. Also, it would be fair that the different expectations premeditated on rumors do not bring harmful prejudices that can trigger dissatisfaction, fear, or anxiety. In an environment in which most people have wrongly formed opinions associated with hostile prejudices, there are few who express differences in judgments, which are openly based on goodwill and rational conclusions. The source of antagonistic prejudices is usually fueled by feelings of insecurity and inferiority that are often adopted from the family environment. In such cases, envy for someone who has proven successful is

associated with defamation masked by hostile prejudices, which are spread in the social environment as forms of revenge. No one is exempt from being subjected to prejudice, but it is advisable for everyone to diminish preconceived opinions and not to make wrong assumptions based on impressions that are not supported by evidence. In extreme cases, intolerance to the way of thinking of others about race or religion is expressed through bigotry, which is the form of hostile prejudice with the greatest power of defamation that can cause damage to the character of the others.

51. As people live in families, communities, and societies, they have obligations to each other as well as to the established order of governance. Everyone has the obligation to contribute to the well-being and prosperity of others through the efforts one can prove and by assuming the responsibilities that must be fulfilled. However, when one assumes the determination to achieve a goal through a process of change or to maintain relationships on a stable platform, the obligation becomes a commitment and is sustained by moral duty. Making

a commitment involves dedication to serve a cause or includes fidelity, honesty, attachment, and affection for a person who has demonstrated similar qualities. Commitment is not a fundamental trait of the human race. There are few people who take on the burden of overcoming inherent obstacles while maintaining in the same time the necessary integrity when deciding to pursue a goal. Before making a commitment decision, one has to carefully consider the conditions under which changes with unexpected results can occur, and the mere desire for dedication could become insufficient. Commitment to a cause or to a person is valuable only when the intended purpose has the merit of including sacrifices and excludes the likelihood of disappointment. Commitment to oneself requires an exact knowledge of the power of achievement based on the will to succeed in overcoming the most difficult obstacles. The fulfillment with excellence of a commitment to self represents the highest satisfaction and the most important principle of success.

52. In the years of childhood we are told how to behave, how to learn, how to

understand, and how to become useful to others and to ourselves. During the time, our experiences come along with different character models from which we have the opportunity to choose one that we consider the closest to our nature. We do not know if the character we have is real or is only imagined and only desired by us as the most appropriate, until we are in a position to see how the traits we have formed are put to test. In the best cases, and under normal circumstances, we are satisfied when we prove consideration, generosity, friendship, and understanding for the needs of others. We consider to have a strong character when the moral beliefs that we have built up over the years prove that we have a fair behavior in all circumstances, even if we are not observed by others when we act or intend to make a decision. The most important trait that shows us that we have a stable character based on a sum of values is integrity. It is the predominant trait of the personality that encompasses all the human values. To have character of integrity means to be permanently devoted to the moral principles that represent the ideal model to be followed in the course of life. To live with integrity means to serve with faith the highest values that guide every step and every decision that one takes and which is confirmed to be fair by one's own conscience.

53. I understand good people who have shown gentleness, kindness, care, and consideration for others. They probably grew up in a positive climate in which parental care, guidance and support were prevalent. During the time those children grew under the beneficial influence of the school, of their friends, of the members of the community, and became constructive elements that made significant contributions to the development of the society. I understand also the evil people who have proven enmity, anger, hatred, and total disregard for others. They probably grew up in a turbulent climate where the positive influence of parents has been lacking since the beginning. During the time, those children became acquainted with others from similar dysfunctional families, and they formed as adults in an environment dominated by disorder, confusion and aggression, becoming a permanent threat to society. Nevertheless, I do not understand

indifferent people who show a complete lack of interest, care or sympathy for others, or even antagonistic feelings. Perhaps they grew up in a positive climate that they later detached from, or perhaps from the beginning they grew up in an unfavorable environment that annihilated their sense of humanity. During the time, they probably went through critical experiences that deepened their feelings of alienation and which caused a sense of a permanent apathy from which they can no longer detach. People pass by them without approaching them, without looking for them, and just avoid them, because indifference transformed especially into apathy, is the accompaniment of an inert soul.

54. At any stage of life we withstand a past that gradually forms as time goes by. We continuously maintain the connection with the past we have lived by analyzing the experiences and commitments that determined the decisions we've made in different stages of our existence. It is necessary to resort to our memories when we encounter similar situations that arise in the present and we can choose

by comparison the most appropriate solution that proves to be currently beneficial. At the same time, it is not a favorable suggestion to apply the method of replacing the present tense with the past, since the actual circumstances are different. Sometimes the experiences of the past disclose emotional states, which are stronger than those of the present are, and then the past we have lived appears much more intense than the realities of the present time. No fact of the past can be brought back with the same force with which it has unfolded in the times that have elapsed. The insistence on withdrawing those events that faithfully are recalled by our memory is not a benefit, but becomes a hindrance in resolving the present situations. It is correct to admit that to a large extent the present time is the result of the actions, choices, and experiences of the past, but the present time is the one that determines the reality based on current needs and on decisions that will influence and decide the future.

55. Experts in social sciences say that during the millennial evolution, humanity could not have reached the maturity of today without the intervention of conflicts. They

seem to be right. A peaceful, comfortable world, without a race of competitions, based on mutual understanding between people and nations, would have become, during the time, a place of languished life and without perspective. The conflict has existed since the appearance of man and became a hereditary trait. As long as the conflict does not become a danger to life, it is necessary as an incentive and strength in existence. The conflict initially appears as a necessity in the simple competition for affirming an opinion based on the desire to achieve success and merit to attain a goal; it occurs when individuals have different opinions, needs, and interests that cannot be resolved by a middle way; it appears as a form of antagonism accentuated when it manifests itself in favor of a new ideology; it is the means of confrontation in the struggle of domination between social classes, ethnic groups, organizations with prevalence of control over those who express opposition; it is a fanatical intolerance towards religious groups; it is a dispute maintained by enmity between people who claim the same rights over certain possessions; on a large scale, it is the armed struggle between two nations, sustained by violence, destruction and death. If people could restrict themselves to mere competitive arguments, humanity would become a safe place for existence. Unfortunately, the tendency of confrontation through violent conflict will never go away.

56. You were harshly reprimanded for the mistake you made in the work for which you were responsible. You were silent and you did not rebel against the harsh words that were addressed to you, because you accepted with dignity that you were wrong and acknowledged your mistake. You held back the tears that were about to flow, and you showed no sign that you endured a humiliation that may not have been fully justified. You went home and in total solitude you let go off on tears that started to flow and you released the bitterness that overwhelmed you. Where was your dignity? Only in the mirror. Dignity is a coat that covers the feelings of humiliation in front of those who caused them, and prevents the ridicule of a critical situation; it is one of the main intrinsic values that justify the importance of being human; it is the direct translation of an attitude that

requires respect and consideration; it is the foundation that sustains confidence and self-respect. The violation of human dignity through abuse and force extends on a large scale, up to extremely offensive limits exercised on poor people who are forced to seek food in the rubbish dumped by the overly-saturated. In most cases of this kind, those concerned prefer to endure the state of misery rather than beg for mercy. Pride is a distant cousin of dignity, but it is a trait that appears on the surface without any reservation to be recognized; it is usually the pinnacle of those who have achieved success and are eager to make it known. If dignity and pride could find a common way of expression, the value of human character would probably gain more consideration.

57. People love each other, hate each other, argue, and these traits are part of each person's individuality. Sometimes we like the way of those we deal with, we like their behavior, their way of reasoning, the way they express themselves, the feelings they impress us with, and we have no reluctance to approve and even imitate their behavior. Other times, however, we find enough reasons why people

are not living up to our expectations, and collaboration with them becomes difficult. It is in everyone's tendency to try to influence the character of someone disagreeable and even to attempt to make changes for its improvement. Each person, however, has a character made up of personal considerations, skill, knowledge, and experiences, and no one can change according to the pleasure and imagination of others. The difference of opinion is usually the most pronounced evidence in the contrast between characters, and is a divergence that extends from simple argumentation to a violent conflict. In this case tolerance intervenes which, if exercised wisely, leads to results of communication without difficulties. People do not give up personal opinions easily, and sometimes the insistence of prevalence leads to unexpectedly unpleasant results. Tolerance implies patience, understanding, and respect for the personality of everyone even in the most unpleasant arguments, and eliminates prejudices against those who have different opinions from ours. Being tolerant of one another means accepting the distinctiveness of everyone's character with the merits and shortcomings that each one has and recognizes.

58.   Friends and colleagues organized a party to celebrate the wonderful success you have recently achieved in the project. The hall is full of people who compete to congratulate you and express themselves with words of praise. You look at them and you see no one, you listen to each one and you hear no one. The room is completely empty and you are alone in total silence and stillness. There is no one around you that you can communicate with because there is no contingency between you and those people who show their appreciation for your merits. You arrive home in your modest dwelling where each thing has a precise position in the same spot from the beginning. The loneliness with which you have surrounded yourself is the environment closest to your thoughts and feelings without being a consequence of a possible depression or a burden caused by adverse circumstances. It is the conclusion resulting from many defeats that you had to maintain an open and communicative interaction with those around you who failed to come close to understand what

was important to you. For a long time you worked on your values, you carved them like precious stones, you gave them the essence and colors that you grew up with and became mature. You wanted to make them known by people you liked to approach, but you did not find someone to share what was part of your most valuable beliefs. You have chosen solitude as a refuge in which you are far from anyone; you can seek and find yourself whenever you want, in a world where you are the only one who knows your thoughts and feelings.

59. Ever since we were born we have been learning continuously throughout our life. Learning is a genetic trait that the organism has applied during the evolution process as a fundamental necessity in the success of survival. It is essential to learn about the transformations in the environment, the conditions of adaptation, and the possibilities of avoiding dangers, while maintaining everything that has been useful in the past and is added to the volume of newly accumulated experiences. The knowledge of reality and of people with whom we share a common life, represents a

process of acquiring the cognitive way of life, in association with new behaviors and alternatives that we choose for the optimization of our existence. Learning in any field and applying in practice the information accumulated is a vital necessity for our existence, especially for the degree of expansion of our thinking capacity, and for the acquisition of an increased ability to reason. People who have studied at the level of excellence in the fields of art and science have proven a great intellectual capacity and have contributed to the highest benefits of enhancing and preserving the treasures of human values. Learning eliminates indolence, friction between people, lack of contribution in finding ways to improve livelihoods, and declines the escalating ignorance which is a major hindrance to the development of society. Learning is not only a necessity but also an immense satisfaction when it is associated with beauty, self-discipline, and fulfilling the goals to be achieved.

60. When giving a child a responsibility it must be explained to him its importance and especially the consequences that will follow if he does not fulfill it. It is a basic

lesson on the long journey of growth and maturity. When an adult is given a responsibility, he is required to fulfill it as well as to accept all the consequences in case of failure. Responsibility is entrusted to someone who is considered capable of making decisions and of having the desire for improving changes in unforeseen situations. Personal actions and the attitude that people display towards others are viewed as subjective attributes that become the responsibility of someone else only in cases where disciplinary intervention is required. Everyone who assumes a responsibility has the obligation to keep commitments and not to blame others in cases in which there are difficulties on the way. Fulfillment of obligations in accordance with the statements made before, stimulates respect and consideration, and strengthens relationships of trust. Each of us has responsibilities towards society and we are obliged to fulfill them according to the laws and ethical conduct, without trying to avoid the duties and commitments that determine the common equilibrium. In the same time, personal responsibility towards oneself is categorical, considering that no one can make decisions for others and no one is responsible for the actions or failures of others. Everyone's life is the accumulation of values, experiences, knowledge, and decisions that have been the result of personal responsibility.

61. In this extremely complicated world everyone has problems and nobody is exempt from them. Some people keep silent and consider it an intrusion into their lives if someone tries through questions or allusions to reach their thoughts and feelings. Other people are eager to face the difficult situations they are forced to encounter and are happy when someone is willing to listen to them. There are not always amateurs who have the ability and willingness to listen with tolerance. In these cases, the interlocutor addresses a person who only hears the sounds of the speech but is not attentive to the content of the words, and then the attempt to communicate becomes an event of frustration. Hearing is quite different from listening, especially in conversations that involve attention and require special intervention. Listening requires to interpret accurately and without discrepancy the topic under

discussion, understanding the problem that needs to be analyzed and eventually resolved, as well as a special attention to carefully follow the feelings of the speaker. Also, to listen with interest to the problems of those who call for help, implies respect for their thoughts, feelings, and attitude, especially assuming that their request was based on hesitation and embarrassment. It is always desirable that the problems exposed be addressed with caution and discretion, and to be expected as a favorable outcome. Sometimes, just listening to someone talking is a delectable joy.

62. Motivation is the propellant, which conveys the message toward the achievement of a purpose. Motivation is defined as the process that initiates, guides, and maintains goal-oriented behaviors. Motivation arises from the impulse to obtain momentary satisfaction when the desired object is in the near field, or from the ambition to carry out a project defined as a goal when the process of realization is carried out for a long time. The reasons that determine the movement to fulfill the feeling of wanting to have something are influenced by necessity,

by the way of life, by the social influence, or by the priorities that intervene during the daily requirements. In the first stage of life, motivation of satisfying needs and desires is led by instincts, which are based exclusively on the physical senses that direct the response to actions and reactions. With the passage of time, there appears the reason that initiates the conscious process in expressing motivation, and becomes dominant over the instincts that continue to motivate the actions and reactions stimulated only by reflexes. The highest level of motivation is represented by the desire to achieve the introspective essence based on accumulated values, on knowledge, on loyal behavior towards oneself, and on the strong feeling of being useful to those who need to know that there is someone in their life who do care for them.

63. Everything in nature is movement and evolution. From the first aspects of life that appeared more than three billion years ago, the working of nature has determined by precise orders and laws the feasibility of the conditions of existence for the organisms that have been formed with each step in the evolutionary stages.

Nature has been the source of stabilization and survival of each life form that has appeared successively or simultaneously. It is not known when and by whom she was called "Mother Nature", but it seems to be the most suitable qualification. Nature is the source of existence of all the creatures that exist on Earth, ensuring the potential for sustaining all the organisms through food, air, water, shelter, and the consolidation of the areas of existence in a unified rhythm of life. Nothing in nature is isolated, but everything is related to something close, far away, or just in the stage of being formed. Throughout time, people have learned that nature cannot be dominated by force but must be understood only. We look at her beauty that fascinates us, the colors, the shapes, and the richness of the images that bring us an emotional state of spiritual well being, making us convinced that we owe nature all the support for who we are.

64. Everyone wants to have a quiet, comfortable and worry-free life, and the desire to have what is needed is common to all people. The work that everyone does is not only a support for the existence, but eliminates most of the

material deficiencies, as well as the mental anxiety. Without working, everyone becomes depressed and cannot find the balance essential for living. The need to achieve an objective is the impulse that leads to satisfaction not only material but also mental, and presumably, everyone is able to fulfill it. When the desire to reach a goal becomes ambitious, the ability to concentrate increases with each step, and the satisfaction of achievement becomes a factor that proves a model for the power to reach any other accomplishment in the future. The daily realities are usually understood with more or little effort and the activity of the people is incorporated in the attempt to acquire what they desire without expecting anything other than what they can know. However, everyone needs a vision of an objective in a perspective that brings a different satisfaction and a material or mental reward at a higher level. The ambition to reach that level triggers the strong will to make every effort that one has, and the success achieved represents the satisfaction and the confidence in possibilities unknown until then. Nevertheless, big ambition is the passion of a powerful character; those endowed with it may perform very good or very bad acts. All depends on the belief and behavior which direct them.

65. Each one of us needs the appreciation of others, either for a successfully achieved objective, or for the personal qualities that we have shown in relation to the others. We always need to know that we are valued for who we are, and for our accomplishments that have made even a small contribution to improving one's life. From daily experiences we learn to choose and value the inherited values as well as the ones we have encountered along the way, we chose them for their special significance, and we keep them in our moral heritage. We learn to appreciate the qualities of people, to recognize their merits, and to treat them with high regard. Appreciation means showing our gratitude, recognizing the quality, value, principles or behavior of people, and the significance of the duties they have successfully performed. Those who do not recognize the merits of one's character or the effort made for the work done, hide envy and selfishness. Appreciation is an open door for welcome in relationships with people, and determines the feeling

of contentment and good feeling with oneself.

66. Over the course of human history, millions of books have been written in many of the languages in which the spoken sounds could be transcribed into combined signs that determined a system of communication between people. It is not possible to define exactly what is meant by a "good" book that can be read and accepted by anyone. Each book describes a topic that addresses a category of people or a single person, opening up new possibilities for knowledge and learning. Every author puts effort, concentration, imagination, and assiduous time, to faithfully render thoughts and feelings that motivated a desire to share his work with others. It is said that books as well as friends must be few and well chosen because they always remain faithful. Each book is a new source of information, new ideas, and enrichment of knowledge. With each book read, the mind is active, receptive, and learns to analyze more accurately the circumstances, characters, habits, and variety of human thinking. Every reader who is pleasantly impressed by a book

feels that his soul is enriched with the beauty and calm required when the daily worries seem to be without end. Without written books over the long past time, the development of civilizations would not have been possible, and the fields of knowledge could not have conquered the research areas that led to the evolution of the human mind.

67. I asked my friend if she went already to the polling place to cast her vote. Her answer was: "I live one step above the poverty line and don't pay taxes. Since I cannot bring any contribution to the prosperity of the country, I considered that is only reasonable and honest not to go out there and express my opinions in choosing a resolution on the ballot, or to elect which candidate for the office would be the best. There are many people like me, and everyone is entitled to act according to what is most suitable regarding the extent of integrity that each one is aware of. There are also, many people who couldn't care less about this subject, but they do cast their vote only because of the legal entitlement they have. My sense of righteousness proved

to guide my conscience, and I couldn't do any other way." I agreed with her.

68. People act differently when they have to make a decision in solving a situation. Some hurry and choose a solution based on superficial information that may be incorrect, while others do research that is more detailed and wait to see results that can be proven correct. Patience implies the ability to expect a favorable situation while revealing an attitude of self-control that prevents the expression of annoyance even in the face of provocation. Making any decision requires a slow step, detailed reflection, and patience that supports flexibility in any commitment. Each action requires thoughtfulness to avoid the occurrence of mistakes that may later prove irretrievable. The need to be patient proves to be the most favorable factor in making an important decision while the haste to solve a problem proves to be a resolution that can lead to failure. Patience is considered a virtue because it is part of the qualities of the character that are gradually assimilated from experiences and relationships with people. Patience is especially necessary in accepting people as they are and encourages tolerance

towards attitudes and opinions that differ from ours. In an extremely complicated world in which anyone and everyone incite anger, patience generates empathy and understanding.

69. All creatures that exist are born to be active. Above all, the human being is endowed with the faculty to analyze perspectives of life, of situations, of daily problems, and based on them, to make plans for the future. People study, research, learn, acquire knowledge, and understand the needs of achieving well-defined goals. When boredom occurs, the human mind begins to languish and the roads to any activity are closed. It seems that any kind of stimulation is no longer capable of inciting any interest, enthusiasm or the desire to be active in even the most diluted form of expression. The causes that usually give rise to boredom come in most cases from repetitive, unproductive but necessary work, and which does not present new perspectives where the imagination could successfully intervene. People who are overwhelmed by the feeling of boredom become vulnerable and inclined to be affected by anxiety, depression,

fatigue, and difficulty to concentrate. Often the state of boredom becomes chronic and manifests itself through the feeling of nullity, which reveals feelings of frustration and helplessness in the face of any attempt of activity. In these cases, the lack of attention and of interest for what is happening around are extended to the maximum and the fatigue and the state of apathy are aggravated. In a word, boredom can be defined as a disease of the mind and soul that rejects any joy and achievement in life.

70. Not everybody can overcome fear all the time. Courage is not a trait with which we are born, but is gradually learned throughout life from circumstances that appear unfavorable and require direct confrontation. Fear, physical or moral pain, dangers in the face of injustice, uncertainty about existence, are factors that stimulate the courage to fight and defeat them. Courage is not necessarily a distinguishing attribute of people who have proven to be strong in character and have proven to be fearless in dangerous situations or in situations that required unexpected interventions. Brave people are usually the ones who primarily trust

in themselves, believe in moral values, are confident in meeting challenges, and intervene without fear in actions that require the risk to face dangers, which threaten them or those close to them. Courage is also demonstrated in situations in which the requirement to participate in a physical or intellectual competition occurs, and when the contenders are driven by the desire to succeed and to obtain personal satisfaction. The lack of courage does not necessarily mean cowardice, but it is closely determined by an insufficient perception of the facts, as well as by absence of understanding and knowledge of the reality that requires an inevitable intervention. Essentially, the courage inherent in daily existence is an essential value that strengthens the individual personality in confrontations which require bravery, and which usually inspire fear of action.

71. The experiences we go through teach us the mechanism we react to circumstances, the way we behave towards others, the way we accept the thinking and actions of the people we collaborate with, or whom we are forced to face, as well. We accumulate new perceptions, feelings,

and driving trends that we analyze and adopt in shaping our behavior toward people and events. The complexity of the system in which we think and react determines the formation of our attitude, which is expressed in the relationships we have or that determines initiatives in meeting situations, which need to be resolved. Daily realities teach us to cooperate with every success or downfall we experience and to adopt an attitude that does not impair our beliefs, values, and motivations. The reaction to respond positively or negatively to a person or situation depends only on choosing how the right attitude becomes controllable and decisive. Emotional states, the predisposition to react positively or negatively, the way of thinking, are factors that determine the behavior and tendency to act towards anyone and everything that intervenes in our life. Confidence in the correctness of a right behavior undoubtedly establishes the feeling of self-confidence, and the conviction in our ability to master an appropriate attitude in any circumstance.

72. Any existing creature is born with the instinct of curiosity that over time has

proven to be a powerful support for survival. Above all, the human being is endowed with the faculty of thought, which makes the feature of curiosity to be developed in a wide area especially when applied in the abstract realm considered to be unlimited. The more we observe and know, the more we understand, learn and want to find new branches of knowledge that are related to everything which might present new possibilities of realization. Curiosity is a need that is constantly asserted and requires to be fulfilled either as new discoveries in improving the existence, or as exploits in the philosophical and scientific field for understanding the way of thinking with applicability in the daily existence. Over time, the primitive instinct of curiosity has developed into the need to investigate new fields of knowledge about the environment that is constantly changing and that requires the adoption of more complex possibilities to improve our existence. Curiosity helps in knowing people's behavior and through fair considerations defines the relationships of collaboration or confrontation, identifying the values and principles of those who are in a position to be analyzed.

The human mind is constantly in search for new findings and never satisfied with enough knowledge.

73. Nature is constantly changing according to the laws established since the beginning of existence. Nothing remains static in its development and evolution while movement makes it possible to grow new elements that appear and enrich all the natural resources. In human society, the change from one situation to another is the dominant factor in the development process, not only for the gradual affirmation of the new requirements that intervene, but also for ensuring the needs that will appear in the future. Change is essential in personal life as well as in social life. Without change, one cannot affirm progress, experience, knowledge, learning, and one cannot anticipate prospects of achieving an existence that will improve the imperative needs of life. Some people resist attempts at change because of fear of failure or because a lack of desire to change the conditions in which they have become accustomed to live without feeling the need for any improvement. The tendency to change is not easy to overcome, because first of

all, there is a predisposition to defend the elements that constitute the habit and which is reluctant in front of the new elements that appear. When people become convinced of the need for making a difference in an existing state or condition, they gradually accept the new changes that help move forward and the variations that occur become a new source of satisfaction and understanding of the diversifications that have occurred.

74. A young boy breaks a vase and tells his mother that his little sister broke it. The mother believes him and reprimands her daughter who starts crying and cannot defend herself. The boy is satisfied and enjoys a feeling of relief. Grown-ups are not different from children when they do mistakes and blame someone else. They just want to keep the focus off them and avoid the frustration that might bring an unpleasant outcome. Blaming someone is easier and simpler than taking responsibility for an unsuccessful action. People who blame others for their mistakes are indifferent to the consequences that come after, and show no remorse when those blamed are punished. Recognizing mistakes becomes

a difficulty when the mind refuses to accept the consequences that follow and that can aggravate an unpleasant situation. Taking responsibility is the attribute of an honest character that is revealed in any difficult circumstance in which the mistakes made are exposed without fear of being criticized or punished. In many cases, people who show a strong character take responsibility for deeds that others have committed but have not had the courage to accept it, and who proved weakness out of fear to expose themselves to serious repercussions. It is a merit of those determined to defend and protect those who cannot protect themselves, and it is a rare quality that is rewarded only by self-satisfaction.

75. Your boss gives you a project to fulfill because he appreciates your knowledge and ability to do it. However, after reviewing the importance and weight of the job, you hesitate in moving forward and you tell your boss that you don't have enough experience to do it. The assignment is given to your colleague who carries out the task with big success and is rewarded. What you really proved was insecurity, lack of self-confidence,

and fear of failure. Self-confidence is imperative to meet with certainty any change that occurs and any event that requires personal involvement. We do not know in advance what will be the result of the action we take, but with confidence preparing the possibilities to resolve the situation, we have at least the certainty that we have tried the path of success through everything we know from experience and learning. In this way we can prove the will to achieve what at first we found difficult for our ability. In order to strengthen self-confidence, it is first necessary to be convinced that we have respect for ourselves and for the values we cherish and which prove our strength of character. When we know how to appreciate the qualities and abilities of our character, we gain the feeling of confidence in the possibilities of success in difficult situations and also the feeling of security in achieving an objective that requires unusual efforts.

76. Personality dictates the way one behaves, acts, and deals with consequences. Cause and effect are strongly linked together and there is no mistake that one is related to the other. Perspectives inspire needs

followed by a plan to fulfill a project, which will end up in success or failure. The outcome will show if the purpose intended to thrive attained the efforts involved in its achievement, and will show the consequences which have been assumed to come after. From an early age, we learn to distinguish what is good from what is harmful. Along the way, we learn to anticipate the favorable or unfavorable results of our actions and if we are equipped with conscience and responsibility, we stop taking actions that can cause personal injury or harm to others. The way in which everyone accepts the consequences of actions, differs according to the way in which each one understands to face the mistakes or the successful fulfillment of a goal. The transition from cause to effect is not always accurately predicted, and cannot be correctly analyzed before the action is completed. We can evaluate in advance the result of our thinking that leads to the achievement of the goal and we can assume in advance the consequences that follow, but we cannot diminish or change them if we are aware that we are making a mistake. The results of our actions have a strong influence on our character, producing either improvement or damage, but never slip away without touching it.

77. Each individual is different from all the others and behaves as such when alone. Nevertheless, most of the people like to be in a small or a big crowd and love to be part of it. Individuality becomes concealed and slowly starts fading away, since a crowd represents an accumulated personality made of individual mixtures and confusions. More and more people run away from their own self by living outside their own distinctiveness, preferring to adopt ideas, feelings, and behavior from those around. Very few people choose the solitude in which they can develop their individuality without restrictions and without being submitted to the social conformity to fit into a certain group. Individuality is formed since the years of youth according to the way in which everyone is affected by the way of understanding and adopting influences from the environment. With age and experience, each person's identity is enriched by filtering the characteristics that correspond to moral values, needs, and predominant interests in defining

individual principles of behavior. People who chose solitude were usually those who usually showed new visions, ideas, and courage in terms of improving the quality of life, accomplishments, and social prosperity. Those who proved a strong individuality and have understood the essential importance of self-knowledge that involves the power to influence and maintain the paths of individual and common progress have always initiated strong human values.

78. If a pet can learn discipline, so can a child, and so can an adult. Discipline is mandatory for better communication, better relationship, and most of all for avoiding lack of consensus. Parents, family, and society establish disciplinary rules to be obeyed, not to be broken, and which are meant to make discipline a practice of habit. Most important in this regard is to cultivate self-discipline, which is an imperative requirement for the growth of self-esteem, to show strength in making right decisions, and not to give up a hard way for achieving an objective. People interpret the discipline in different ways and act according to personal initiative that appears, and

which is differently translated. The lack of interest in assessing circumstances, the lack of power to act and to assume responsibility, lead to a total renunciation of the efforts and of the persistence to achieve even the most insignificant goals. We are not born with a sense of discipline and we do not know it until we begin to learn and practice it in all the actions we take as well as in all the relationships we have. Over time, the sense of discipline becomes routine and manifests itself as a conventional habit without any conscious intervention. Self-discipline builds a better character, is rigorously needed in the stability of thinking power, in balancing emotions through self-control, and in preventing addictions that could eventually affect the organism and its health.

79. Being kind to one another is not that hard as people might think. A gentle touch, a warm feeling, a soft word, are expressions of kindness that most of honest people show to others, without expecting anything in exchange. However, there are also many people who exhibit the same conduct with hope to reach the sensitivity of someone who can

reward them or whom they intend to use for reaching a certain scope. Those are hypocrites who never fall short of means of taking advantage in any situation in which good and decent people happen to be in their way. Kindness has no price but only value. When there is a desire to make it known, kindness is reflected in everything people think and do. In many circumstances, kindness is interpreted as a trait of naïve and weak people, and this is extremely wrong; being kind, generous, and considerate, often requires the intervention of courage and the power of confrontation when such expressions are interpreted as pity or falsehood. Anyone, eventually, can learn and accept the impressive value of kindness, which has the power to transform behavior and mode of thinking. Care and kindness awaken the empathy that develops and explains the confused feelings of those who suffer; both make possible to understand the causes that produced sadness or depression, and to help in the search for a solution of relief. People who are admired for their mind and loved for their kindness make a better place of this world.

80. The word "climate" has different meanings. When referring to weather conditions it's easy to understand that if it's cold or stormy outside, you have to wear warm clothes, while when it's hot you can wear a bathing suit and nobody cares. At the same time, when climate refers to family ambience, if you are born from decent, hard working parents, you learn about behavior, values, get a good education, and become a productive person. If you are born in a dysfunctional family, you might be abused, don't get anything from what is needed to grow up properly, you run away, and shortly after you become a despondent. Next, is the society's climate, crammed with rules and regulations that you dislike but have to obey. Then, comes the climate of friendship, which gives a large area of feelings and emotions that not always are favorable to sustain a strong relationship. Usually, friends are casual acquaintances, who meet over diner for a pleasant conversation, then they go apart making superficial promises to see each other again perhaps next month, and forget all about you because there are no bonds, no memories to share, and no concern for each other's well being. A true friend

is like a deep green emerald, amazingly valuable, rare, and precious. You both help each other through thick and thin, you share memories, feelings and thoughts, and you both make sacrifices to put each other first. If you can find such a friend, consider yourself as being blessed.

81. It is not easy to accept a failure. The efforts made to carry out a project, the long time required, the difficulty of the research done, the ambition to achieve success and compensation, all these collapsed due to mistakes that crept in and could not be prevented. The result of dissatisfaction to fail was a nervous breakdown that contributed to a decrease in self-confidence and a desire to give up any further attempt to achieve. The fear of a new failure becomes strong and prevents any effort to initiate a plan to develop a new goal. An invisible threat of failure prevents the tendency of being exposed to new situations that might affect a correct judgment of the ability to achieve. Loss of control over the will to try again leads to an inefficacy in finding a solution to overcoming problems that affect negativity and fear. From mistakes and from the experiences of the issues

encountered, over time appears a new approach of searching for success that will be applied in achievements with new challenges. From these, emerge self-respect and confidence in the power of accomplishment that have been inactive and covered by failures. The newly acquired positive feelings about oneself invigorate the courage to face with strength situations and challenges similar to those encountered before, which caused failure followed by pessimistic consequences.

82. The daily situations we encounter and the needs that arise with each problem to be solved, give us the ability to choose the most appropriate solution that meets the objective considered. The choice we make depends on the perspective of a successful achievement in the future, on the knowledge of the factors that influence the accomplishment without difficulty of the goal, as well as on the consequences that could bring success or failure. Everyone is free to choose from the multitude of possibilities considered most suitable for a solution with convenient premises that can ensure a satisfactory outcome. The events and

circumstances encountered daily or occasionally determine how we may or may not know our power to judge exactly the correct choice of a solution to solve a current problem as well as the possibility to predict a future dealing with a similar problem. From the strange potpourri of human characters as well as from the mixture of simple or complicated situations that occur simultaneously, a correct choice becomes decisive in the accurate continuation of relationships as well as in solving useful goals. Each choice we make at a given time, determines favorable or adverse consequences that further determine the attitude we will take regarding relationships with people as well as in the activities we will continue to face. From experience, mistakes, and successes, we learn to make rational choices with safer and more efficient results. The consequences following the choices we make today are reflected in everything we do later, as well as in our behavior, which stands for the responsibilities assumed as a result of our acts committed with success or failure.

83. In this medley world in which we live there are still good people. Compassion, generosity, altruism, empathy, are characteristic features of those who understand the sufferings of others and offer them without expecting any compensation from people who need them. The poor, the sick, the disadvantaged are helped by people who see and understand their feelings, lack of perspective, their desires and needs. The quality of being good is hereditary and either develops with the accumulation of experiences and the passage of age, or disappears when the conditions of life become precarious and people become selfish, incorrect, and careless in the face of the difficulties of their peers. Humanity has survived over time thanks in particular to people who have helped each other and faced together the vicissitudes of life with the courage and care they have shown each other in stressful situations. Help is not always asked for, but rather people who need help hide their feelings that overwhelm them and that they consider too embarrassing to be revealed. Help comes from those who recognize the needs of others and do not wait to be asked to provide it,

but understand without explanation the urge to intervene. They show a desire to improve the deplorable condition that they observe and that seems to be unresolved. The help offered usually is even more beneficial when the will to help oneself arises in the attitude of the person in question. Also, people who assist others help themselves at the same time, through the contentment they have and which gives them the satisfaction of a just motivation and an increased self-esteem.

84. A smooth road is in front of you, inviting you to enjoy a refreshing walk, but your feet are bleeding and you cannot walk. Happiness is sometimes all around you, inviting you to enjoy every minute of it. You cannot experience the pleasure of it, because your soul is bleeding and your mind is overwhelmed with anguish. Only someone who dearly cares about you can bring you the alleviation you are looking for and that you cannot reach. A gentle touch, a warm word, a kind voice, will bring you a sigh of comfort and will give you no less than a feeling of contentment by having a true friend who relieves your anguish, helping you

to cope in situations of uncertainty. If not happiness, at least an emotional state of fulfillment will come along to give you a peaceful ease of mind and quietude to your troubled soul.

85. Disagreements are everywhere in the world from the smallest all the way up to fights and wars. Differences of opinion at first seemingly harmless, escalate to the level of conflict when neither side gives in to the intention to defend their point of view. Conflict affects family relationships, friendships, and good understanding between those who collaborate in activities that involve achieving a goal. Disputes are accentuated in situations where interests, qualification of values, and essential needs that require imminent action become causes of antagonism. The collision between hostile parties sets off emotional reactions that can manifest through anger, hatred, and a desire to do harm. Hatred is said to be the attribute of people with the lowest degree of culture. This is not always the case when only those lacking education and culture are hostile to people who denote superior qualities and values. There are countless people with an exceptional degree of

culture who prove to be full of malice and the desire to harm others, either out of envy in the pursuit of success, or out of hostility against lack of appreciation, or out of memories of traumas that never healed, or for many other reasons that require a simple spark to set off anger and hatred. In many cases, hatred is triggered when the one who manifests it observes traits from his personality in the character of the opponent and does his best to exterminate what appears to be exclusive possession, unwanted to be shared with someone else. Hatred is a dormant feeling that everyone has, but which is triggered only to those who cannot control themselves and prefer to defeat their opponent by doing harm or by final elimination.

86. We learn good and bad habits and make them part of our behavior. Some are inherited, some are acquired, some make life more pleasant, and some make life miserable. Habits are not objectives but are the way we treat objectives through repetition aimed at a special activity that excludes additional efforts to think. Discipline and self-control become necessary in the process of forming

habits, but they develop in parallel with repetition only until the habit becomes automatic and manifests itself as a routine outside of consciousness. The habits that have proven to be beneficial facilitate the constant appeal to the initiative to make decisions in daily activities that do not require special attention. Some habits are useless but once they are already acquired, it is difficult to give them up, such as carrying an umbrella all the time, whether it is raining or not. Some habits are acquired from activities that are rarely performed but out of useful measures, they are adopted and become part of the behavior. Often some people possess qualities and goods that others lack, and the habit of sharing them becomes an attribute that brings satisfaction and increases the desire to help and take care of the needs of others. A habit that is useful becomes beneficial in the development of physical and mental health and contributes to raising the level of discipline and self-control. Good habits make daily activities much easier, making life possible without the need to consume additional mental effort and time necessary to reach an achievement.

87. Nobody knows who came up with the word "happiness". Perhaps someone who experienced a stronger feeling than thrill, or perhaps someone who envisaged a mental picture of an emotion to transcend elation. Anyway, happiness is a strong feeling when living a moment fully, lasts a very short time, and then is archived into memories. There is no exact term to define happiness, but in simplistic terms, it can be said that although it is a mystery, happiness is a feeling of contentment caused by the full satisfaction of a gratified purpose, love, and hope in achieving what is desired. Life must be considered as it is, and all that is good, generous, and compatible with human values must be gathered, cherished, and considered gratifying enough to qualify happiness. When the satisfaction of needs is fulfilled, the strong desire and the determination to succeed in the future, opens a wide path, without obstacles, for a vision of happiness that can appear and that can bring a feeling of extreme self-satisfaction. Many small gratifications and moments of joy go unnoticed or are neglected due to lack of consideration, and although they do not reach the level of happiness, they are important enough

to motivate a state of contentment that should be treasured. People who know the mere potential of social relations, the minor importance of the accumulation of material goods, as well as the insignificant utility of superficial pleasures, give up seeking happiness outside their sphere of thought and limit themselves to the possibilities of seeking and building it in themselves.

88. The cultural core of a nation or ethnic group is built by the totality of individual and societal values, which in turn are based on the cultural treasure of the ancestors. Culture is specific to each nation or ethnic group and is displayed from simple speech and customs to works of art, literature, philosophy, and science, followed by all the elements of societal superstructure. Culture includes people's way of life, way of thinking and expressing, feelings, religious beliefs, perspectives in achieving goals, and the formation of values that lead to continuous individual and societal development. Tradition is an essential factor in assimilating the culture passed down from previous generations on which the formation of new concepts of

societal organization is based, as well as in increasing the individual level to expand the possibilities of knowing concrete facts and abstract thinking. Cultural development leads to the conception of superior models of thinking that allow the increase of the mental capacity determined by education, knowledge, and experience. Every nation and every ethnic group is faithful to a certain set of values with which they grew up, in which they believe, and which categorically must be respected by all other cultural authorities. The different cultures that meet internationally contribute to the improvement and quality of life, through learning new possibilities of understanding by increasing tolerance, through exchanges of experience and knowledge, and through mutual adoption of distinct values.

89. People always want to have something, to do something, to find something new and useful, or to overcome and eliminate the difficulties that always arise. Desire is an impulse that manifests itself through the need to obtain what could meet a demand determined by imperative or transient circumstances. When the

perspective of the fulfilled goal is seen as a success, its transformation into reality proves that the impulse which determined the initiation of the reason for action was correct. Desire can pursue the satisfaction of a productive goal or is manifested obsessively, in which case it becomes uncontrollable, is exercised as predominance in action, and is minimized as a goal. The intensity of desire sometimes becomes overwhelming, insistent, demanding, tenacious, and there are not many people who manage to have control over its negative action that could affect behavior or that could have detrimental effects on self-confidence. Everyone wants to have communicative and friendly relationships with others and everyone tries to make every effort to achieve an acceptable collaboration. Usually, everyone's inclination is to contribute with goodwill, consideration, and respect for the comfort or desires of others, without imposing themselves with hostile opinions determined only by the impulse to prove a false superiority over others. When desires, no matter how intense, are coordinated efficiently and harmoniously, they emphasize the beneficial power of feelings and involve the ability to achieve a constructive goal.

90. Ideas are never in shortage to people, at least to those who still can think. The brain takes every bit of information, processes it, and gives birth to good, bad, interesting, useful, or unworthy ideas. The experience generates new ideas in the elaboration of concepts and protects the correct development of the new variables that intervene in the process of formation and achievement of the goal. A new idea in the elaboration of a concept is motivated by the need to improve an existing cause, and is justified by results that prove progress in obtaining an outcome with superior quality. Individual and societal development is based on new ideas that appear as a need to replace the old ones and which, through the elaboration of concepts, form the support for progress in the maturation of thinking and in the constant search for methods of improvement. New suggestions are triggered by conditions, facts, or aspirations. In addition, communication between people and the interest in knowing the way of thinking of others lead to new information that assemble

new perspectives with useful points of view in finding new ideas. Also, mental exercises involve factual propositions that are inherent in the description of events or characters that could mimic the reality by a vivid imagination. The highest level of thinking is the ability to develop abstract ideas that are triggered by external stimuli captured by sensory organs and transposed to a higher plane. The faculty of the mind to select a unique path or a new way to achieve a certain goal is related to abstract thinking that has reached the highest degree of development in people with exceptional intelligence. Without abstract thinking, humanity would have remained at an obscure level, and civilization would have been at a minimal degree of development.

91. Common sense is a tiny feature with great power. It is said that it is triggered by intuition and not by logic, which is why very intelligent people put it aside and neglect it. It is a simple form of decision making, especially since it has the ability to predict the consequences of an action, even if taken differently by each person. Common sense is based on experience and long practice of avoiding errors that

may occur in difficult or similar situations to those known before, and which have been successfully resolved by applying practical and simple decisions. In daily activities, pragmatic problems appear at every step and their solution is facilitated by applying the learning of methods based on recognizing the consequences met in previous cases. Common sense is understood and accepted by anyone who is capable of a sound judgment, sufficient to recognize a situation that does not seem to be solvable by specialized knowledge, but which can be solved without difficulty by applying the practice learned from experience. People are not born with this trait, but throughout their lives, they learn it from circumstances that arise and that determine the choice to solve problems by simply applying sound judgment or by looking for a solution based on expertise. The ability to easily interpret the answer to a problem, when complications arise and difficulties seem inherent, is an indispensable quality to perceive the consequences, to understand the most appropriate solutions, and to share them with other people who go through similar experiences.

92. One of the basic characteristics of all creatures is the communication between them. We are all born with this trait but only people acquire the ability of speaking by learning words and language. At an early age, communication is manifested through sounds, gestures, and emotional states that represent needs. Word learning takes place gradually and the accumulation of speech is accentuated with age. Without communication, people would not be able to share ideas, feelings, knowledge, information, and especially would be unable to establish relationship with each other. The development of humanity and different cultures since ancient times, have been possible by assimilating the information shared between communities, ethnic groups, nations, and personalities who have worked to achieve common goals. People are different in how they perceive the realities of life which makes communication difficult when divergence in opinions intervene, distance in relationships occurs, and behavior is affected. Besides understanding, an important factor in the way of communication is listening carefully and appreciating the topics discussed without

causing interruptions that can offend the speaker. The way of personal and social communication in today's society has developed through the expansion of modern technology that provides all the possibilities of contact at the greatest distances, in the shortest time, and with an exceptional accuracy. In addition to all these, people avoid loneliness and seek to be close as much as possible to each other.

93. It is said that people are different and they should be respected just the way they are. Perhaps so, but this affirmation doesn't work for me. This is a statement mentioned probably in school books to teach the young generation respect for the adults, no matter what they do or what they talk. I cannot respect ignorant people who no matter if they are poor or rich, they all had the opportunity to get at least a basic education. I cannot respect abusive people who use power to beat up, insult, and hurt physically and morally the others. I cannot respect cruel people who torture and kill. I cannot respect people who promote racism and hatred. I cannot respect people whose most concern in life is only to make money while using dishonest methods and taking advantage

of those who trusted them. I cannot respect people who betray friendship and profit from consideration, generosity, helpful feelings, and kindness. I cannot respect people who lie, cheat, swindle, exploit, and have total disregard for laws. I cannot respect people who don't understand any of the societal problems but provoke violent public disturbances, just to make a mockery of the authorities, and to entertain themselves. I can only respect people who are able to teach me how to become better, how to enlarge my understanding about life, how to gain confidence about myself, how to never do harm. I can only respect people from whom I can learn what consideration, kindness, generosity, and human values are. I can only respect people who made me find a correct reason to act, who made me feel proud of my work, and who opened for me new perspectives that I can achieve, cherish, and share with people I love.

94. To be honest means to directly expose unobstructed thoughts and feelings that would hide duplicity, superficiality, and deception. In many cases, however, sincere expression of opinion about others

in front of them can cause dissatisfaction, anger, and broken relationships. It is a kind of semi-honesty that is expressed and that involves a degree of hypocrisy. So why honesty is considered one of the greatest values of human character, since it cannot always be expressed insofar as it should represent the truth? Perhaps only because it is already included in the package of values that represent generosity, consideration, and self-respect. Not everyone can accept sincerity without analyzing the reason that determined its expression, and without being completely convinced of the accuracy of the thoughts and feelings that contributed to its affirmation. People who know the importance of sincerity and know that often being honest in relationships with others is not the right attitude, prefer to refrain from expressing their thoughts or feelings, and choose silence. It is much better to avoid being honest than to express honesty disguised as hypocrisy. If sincerity cannot be asserted in full understanding and acceptance of the situation or subject, it is honorable to find a middle ground on which hypocrisy is avoided. It is extremely important, however, that sincerity be total and without any doubt when it comes to analyzing one's personal thoughts, feelings, and criticism. Maintaining self-respect is based exclusively on honest recognition of achievements and mistakes alike, in which case sincerity acts directly and without obstacles on the conscience.

95. Excellence is the distinction of the analytical mind. Some people are not content with simple or superficial answers in their quest to find the motivation for an action or a fact, but explore all the possibilities and climate that could provide additional information in the smallest detail. The analytical mind is the laborious result of the efforts exerted over time in order to achieve the superlative in interpreting perspectives and in fulfilling aspirations. It is the ability of people who demonstrate an excessive desire to achieve remarkable values and who have proven original possibilities to produce exceptional works. Vast culture, solid education, control over character, tenacity to achieve magnificent values, are attributes that driven by a disciplined mind contribute to the revelation of excellence in all areas where dedication and fidelity are represented

by an unusually strong personality. At the heart of reaching excellence is not only the passion to achieve unusually deserving values, but also the stimulation of intellectual faculties to develop to the maximum the ability to explore in abstract and experimental fields. Philosophy, art, literature, science, flourished and evolved thanks to people who proved excellence in thinking, in aspirations, and in personality. People who have proved excellence have been few in human history, but they have left behind a valuable treasure that has contributed substantially to the development of civilizations. Without their greatness, humankind would have remained at a rudimentary stage of thought and expression, and would never have known the magnificence to which the human mind can reach.

96. We are born to be free, they say. But, are we? Are we saying that we are free only because we are on the other side of the prison walls where those who break the law are incarcerated? That would not be enough to say that we are free. Freedom is a notion that we learn throughout life and whose rules are established in

accordance with the requirements of the code of individual ethics and the regulations of the societal organization. Freedom of expression is a fundamental right and is enshrined in laws that support it within defined limits that cannot be violated. Nevertheless, in a seemingly friendly conversation, we cannot afford to use offensive words to defend our point of view. So freedom of speech is limited by the code of ethics. If we have political opinions that we want to make known, we declare our suggestions in front of the public, but on the condition that we do not use inflammatory words that would be followed by punishment and law. So the freedom to express our political opinions is limited by strict regulations that protect society. People arm themselves for personal protection, but violent incidents occur frequently and those guilty are punished and imprisoned. So freedom of action is limited by the threat of punishment inscribed in the societal order. In all areas of existence, freedom is partial only, and is allowed within limits that cannot be exceeded. However, freedom is not limited by laws and regulations when it becomes a personal action exercised in the field of learning, exchange of useful information, accumulation of moral values, and the development of humane activities. Freedom of thought is unlimited and is the most necessary virtue in the continuous development of personality, consciousness, confidence, and self-esteem.

97. Reading a book is one of the most gratifying pleasures. One cannot even imagine how the development of humanity would have evolved without the existence of books. It is perhaps the greatest blessing mentioned in the millennial history of human evolution. Books have opened new paths to unknown horizons, guided unparalleled perspectives, expanded the possibilities of knowledge and learning, contributed to the development of thought and to enrichment of the soul. Books have become an integral part of people's lives, the most useful source for finding information, the basis for the growth of education and culture, and the means of direct communication of new ideas. There is no unanimous opinion in the appreciation of a book, because everyone has particular preferences and considerations in evaluating the

content and expression of the subject. An interesting book attracts the reader to participate in the action, to keep pace with the development of the characters, and to take part in the exchanges of words and feelings communicated between them. The reader becomes a participant in the action and a collaborator with the author's intentions in analyzing the characters' behavior, their reactions, and their relationships, as the evolution of the action amplifies and contributes to understanding the motivation that led to the initiation of the work. A book is not only a mode of educating people and growing of culture, but it becomes a significant factor in finding out the way of thinking, the feelings and aspirations of the author who wanted to share with others a style of thought, which might be useful and interesting. A book that reveals new ideas, intense, intuitive, or spontaneous feelings, and that denotes an affiliation between the writer's way of reasoning and that of the reader, becomes a valuable friend who always remains faithful and reliable especially in moments of loneliness.

98. The individual and societal evolution took place in successive stages throughout the millennial history starting with the first societal organizations and culminating with the civilization of the contemporary, modern era. Simple laws were drafted in the beginning that became increasingly complex to ensure a frictionless development of the economic, cultural, and defense sectors. Each nation that has emerged throughout history has confirmed the identity of a culture that has become known for its aspirations to elevate human values and its desire to share with other nations scientific discoveries, art, literature, philosophy, and concepts for improving the quality of life. Many of the civilizations that have asserted themselves have fallen and disappeared. Our contemporary civilization has reached the peak of development that has followed the industrial revolution. The economic branches have multiplied, the social needs have increased, the differences between classes have accentuated, the frictions between nations have led to the amplification of armament production, especially of weapons of mass destruction, while cultural progress lagged far behind.

However, this synthetic evolution has successfully succeeded in making space flights, genetic mutations for scientific purposes, production of artificial food, medical treatments with countless drugs that destroy the organism, and many other similar inventions. At the same time, the culture broke away from the unity with the general development of the society, it was left far behind and without any possibility to recover. The long-term prospects of the modern civilization look bleak, susceptible to vulnerability, and without hope of advancing for the benefit of humankind.

99. Everyone has a sense of attraction for a person, a pet, a thing, or an idea, depending on the desire to approach or to know the subject. When the interest or temptation to approach is manifested with enough power, the attraction increases and becomes an attachment. Relationships between people who know and appreciate each other lead to the need to share common feelings, consideration, opinions, and loyalty. The physical or moral attraction must be reciprocal and have the same intensity in order to last. When disappointments arise, attachment

begins to crumble and regrets become a burden that is wished to be left behind. Sometimes it dissipates, but sometimes produces suffering that is followed by the desire to isolate oneself and to avoid similar experiences in the future. Friendship is a relationship in which the attraction to the same concerns and the desire to share them brings together people who are capable of mutual trust, reciprocal support, and unconditional loyalty. When insecurity occurs in relationships that are considered stable and unquestionable, friends move away from each other and leave behind a bitter and sad memory, which some despise it and others keep it as a disappointment. The least vulnerable attachment in life is for work. People who have the passion to devote their mental exertion and feelings in the elaboration of a work project become attached to the perspective of successfully achieving the proposed goal. As the work process unfolds, each successful stage becomes a reward that reflects devotion, trust, insight, and satisfaction. Even if the ultimate goal does not bring special rewards and recognition, the dedication that has been constantly active has been an attachment to a cause that has satisfied the mind, soul, and belief in oneself.

100. Beauty is a mirage that entices the senses and accelerates the mind in search of the ideal. Beauty is the basic feature of Creation and life. It is a mirage because it can be seen, it can be felt, but it cannot be touched. All expressions of beauty contain an illusory element of eternity that inspires the approach to perfection and an imaginary ideal that cannot be reached, but that stimulates the vision of greatness. There is no exact definition of beauty but it can be said with certainty that any aspect of it stimulates a feeling of admiration that reflects the desire for a permanent contemplation. Nature exposes its beauty through shapes, colors, movement, and the quintessence of terrestrial life. All existing creatures without exception, even the seemingly ugly ones, have a beauty trait that attracts curiosity and a desire for looking at. People express their beauty through physical or moral traits, or both. The appreciation of a human figure depends on the perception of the senses and on the way in which the visual attractiveness interprets the real image or

a comparative one to a model imagined to be ideal. Physical beauty stimulates an aesthetic feeling but is relative, transient, and short-lived. What fascinates and produces a deep impression is the beauty reflected by the value of feelings and the way in which reason is decisive in the formation of the character. Human values devoted to a balanced system of thinking determine the essence of the moral qualities distinctive for each personality, and the complexity of a disciplined mind. Intrinsic beauty is attained through acquired knowledge, development of intelligence, right choices, consideration for the others, self-respect, and at the bottom line is the ideal that every human being must aspire to and reach for.

101. It was a warm, sunny day, and my three years old son was playing outside, running with the dog and both chasing the cat. In that evening we expected important guests coming for dinner. I asked my son to come inside, gave him a good bath, dressed him nicely and delivered him a lecture about behavior. I told him to control his manners, to speak only when addressed, and to behave like a civilized person. He listened with

patience, and at the end I asked him if he understood what I said. He nodded in agreement, and his only question was if the word „civilized" is spelled with the letter „v" or „f". Seemingly, he didn't pay any attention to my carefully elaborated speech. Much later, he became professor of Art History and Philosophy of Art, at the age when most youngsters start their journey across the field of learning and knowledge. If you want to know how your child's development moves forward, open with him a discussion in a field of knowledge which is at his level of understanding and above, using new words, new expressions, and enticing his curiosity to find new meanings. He will run with a strong desire to learn something different or to show self-confidence in what he already knew, liked, and valued. In a new field of knowledge opened for him to discover the unknown, he will pick-up all the pebbles that come across and dump them in his pockets, and also he will pick-up all the flowers on his road and give them to the person he loves the most.

102. What is equally important to everyone is meeting the needs of food, clothing, and

shelter. Importance is a variable factor and extends on a large scale depending on the needs of each that are different from one case to another. The family is important for everyone to a different degree depending on the stability and relationships that may be conducive to an existence of safety and well-being, or may be destructive in the case of a dysfunctional family. Importance is also a factor dependent on the level of education and culture. For people with a low level of education, priority is given to cheap entertainment, noisy parties, gatherings where drugs are consumed together, and earning a living by the wrong means. For people with an average level of education it is important to increase material well-being in particular, which is supported by the need for a permanent job, acceptable relationships between family members, and maintaining the association with reliable friends. For people with a high level of education, the major importance is directed towards broadening the fields of knowledge, researching unknown territories, enriching moral values, and maintaining family relationships at the highest level of behavior. Also, the choice and maintenance of relationships with friends is rigorously analyzed, which usually ensures a lasting attachment based on mutual trust and loyalty. Especially in this category are people who attach great importance to the development of individual and social values, to self-respect and self-knowledge, as well as to introspection that allows the permanent assessment of mental and emotional development.

103. People experience all kinds of emotions every day, from the one with the least significance to the strongest passion. Circumstances and elements of reality trigger physical and mental reactions that produce states of well-being or negatively affect the way we reason in the conduct of behavior, decisions, and social interaction. Emotions that arise from memories trigger moments lived before that have had a strong influence on how the events followed. Bringing them back to the present reality can help to orient in the right direction the way in which reason and feelings are affected. What is most important in triggering emotions is the effort to understand their origin, the spontaneous reaction activated, and consequently the adoption of the

appropriate attitude. In this way, the influence on thinking and feelings can be controlled and lead to favorable results that can beneficially affect the impact on personal attitude and relationships with others. When emotions are triggered by antagonistic forces that incite violence, the immediate reaction without premeditation is the opposition expressed by action or argument with the tendency to defeat not so much the opponent, but especially the sense of inferiority that becomes harmful. Beneficial emotions such as love, happiness, success, open wide the ability to understand and accept self-confidence and the desire to be in permanent relationships with people who contribute to their development. When we analyze the emotions that overwhelm us, we more easily understand the reason that determines their action and the effects that influence the personality, behavior, and commitments in close relationships. The most important attitude is to learn how to control positive and negative emotions at any time when they become staggering.

104. At a given moment, an expected successful result went wrong, and from

there a superstition was born. Next time a similar circumstance will be avoided for fear that a same outcome might come by. Everyone believes in some kind of superstition, not necessarily in a black cat or an inside umbrella, but in occurrences that one time or the other proved to be hostile and therefore had to be avoided. Even the most educated minds are trapped in unpleasant situations and cannot escape from believing that something bad and unexepectadly might hapen and cannot be controlled. In the days of the tribal appearance, people believed in supernatural powers that had the authority to punish any deed that did not please them. The fear of retribution led to the origin of superstitions that were passed on to all generations who continued to respect them. In the same ancient times, the belief in supernatural powers with beneficial intentions led to the belief in the protection of meritorious deeds and in the removal of powers that brought destruction and caused evil. Superstitions in benevolent powers formed the basis of religious beliefs that asserted themselves by adding new interpretations in deities and later in a single absolute power. Superstitions are said to be the religion of uneducated minds, and yet reality disputes this claim. People have ingrained fear in the way they think and react, and no one is exempt from the consequences that can occur when the fear of the unknown becomes dominant. Science over time and religious ideals have failed to eradicate fear and have failed to bring about the improvement of thinking that manifests itself against all evidence to the contrary, and that maintains belief in superstitions. As long as there is ancestral fear, there will be credence in superstitions.

105. It is said that gratitude is the highest human virtue. Since everyone is entitled to an opinion, I am too when saying that if expressed truthfully all virtues deserve the same praise and should not be brought to scale. Gratitude is one of them. A gesture of benevolence addressed directly to someone is usually received with a few simple words of gratitude. When compensation is expected in return, the act of benevolence becomes interest and loses its value. Satisfaction is usually a personal gratification of the giver more than of the one who receives. Reminding people of the good things

done to them is similar to expressing a rebuke that emphasizes the expectation of compensation in addition to the words of gratitude expressed. Existence in common determines the efforts of all together in the realization of the benefits that contribute to the satisfaction of everyone and to which gratitude can be expressed only by promulgating the values that were the basis of inspiration to give more than to receive. Gratitude cannot be requested, demanded or constrained, it can only be given. It is associated with the feeling of satisfaction that determines positive emotions, contributes to the enrichment of useful experiences and is the basis of friendships. What is very important is the feeling of gratitude that people must be aware of for everything they have and they should appreciate the natural and social well-being without the tendency to covet what is not necessary but they would like to have. They do not have to express their gratitude with words, but they have to show and share with others the meaning of those words. Self-satisfaction based on the feeling of security determined by self-sufficiency is decisive in the formation of a strong character that does not allow inflections and distortion in estimating the values of virtues.

106. Questions are like a buffer when the conversation is languishing and the interlocutors start to get bored. People are born with the feature of curiosity that is accentuated from an early age, and each door that is opened with a question leads to finding new knowledge or supplementing with alternative hypotheses what was known before. Education and culture are based on questions that have led to scientific discoveries, philosophical systems of thought, the development of the imagination in the expression of art, and beliefs that have channeled moral values. Questions stimulate thinking and trigger the search for the right solutions in decisions that may present doubts or conflicts when the translation into facts is questionable. The study of reality is based on questions asked by anyone who wants to know the anatomy of events and the progressive development of new perspectives in the formulation of the future. The accessible information proved to be the result of countless questions that arose from the desire to understand and assimilate the knowledge of ideas,

facts, imagination, and achievements that people have developed over time. Human character was analyzed in detail and defined according to studies conducted by researchers who were curious to ask questions about any motivation that manages to explain differences in behavior and how each individual acts differently in similar situations. The common or specific values that people believe in and practice result from questions that have raised doubts and contradictions and have been clarified by comparative criteria based on preferential choice and personal justification. For any question that arouses interest there is somewhere a satisfactory answer, or one unacceptable, or one illusory, or there is no answer at all, but it must be sought continuously with hope that it will be found.

107. In casual conversations, people use sometimes words that are not justified but that fill in gaps in speech, such as "ideal", "perfection", "absolute". These are big words with pleasant resonance and they sound classy. They have a nebulous, illusory understanding, and their interpretation cannot be verified.

For everyone the desired ideal is different and depends on the needs, ability, experiences, and confidence that have to be exercised with determination and effort in achieving the proposed goal. Most people consider the prospects of achieving a flourishing existence and make every effort to reach the ideal they want. For some the ideal is the attainment of a successful career, for others the ideal is to maintain harmonious relationships with family and friends, for others the ideal is to achieve a strong personality through education, culture, and moral values. For each individuality, ideal is the goal considered the highest level one can aspire to, but which still always admits a higher degree of achievement. "Perfection" is an illusory term that some people aspire to but that is never attainable. Life encounters difficulties, mistakes, and insufficient means for a harmonious development, regardless of the immense efforts that are made to correct the deficiencies that occur. Achieving perfection is also impossible, and there is no higher level above it. The term that tries to describe the "absolute" is also illusory, because it is not tangible or on the scale of human aspirations. What can be assumed by the term absolute is an independent model generated from the totality of known realities, deciphered, understood, and accepted, accumulated with the totality of the unknown realities, which are supposed to exist. What still remains, as a high hope is that the excellence of the human mind can discover the unknown and make possible the reach of the farthest limits of understanding it.

108. The feeling of defeat is not easy to take. Years ago, I participated in a contest in which the prize was a vacation overseas. I failed to meet the required conditions and I lost. I was disappointed, sad, and felt ashamed in front of my family and my two best friends who always trusted my potential to attain everything I set out to achieve. What was more disappointing was the attitude of my friends who, using a cordial attitude and words of encouragement, tried to show me empathy, consideration, and make predictions for the future with the assurance that I would succeed in even more difficult competitions. Although it seems contradictory, their attitude instead of having a positive effect on my rather

troubled state, and instead of having a calming effect, irritated me, angered me, and incited an uncontrollable outburst that none of them deserved, and no one was able to explain it. My revolt against the failure I suffered instead of diminishing by the obvious display of the warm feelings expressed by my friends, worsened to the point of my decision to isolate myself. I was on the verge of breaking a lasting friendship for many years in which affection, respect, and mutual trust were blameless. I realized later that the state of irritation I had gone through was due to the dissatisfaction of being looked at a degrading level with which I was not accustomed and which in those moments triggered a feeling of compassion close to pity. After long reflections, I realized that my attitude of revolt was not directed towards the kindness and affection of my friends who were trying to comfort me, but was directed towards myself who could not accept failures and disappointments. I understood that the peace I was looking for was only in my ability to have it by accepting the unpleasant situation I had gone through and by acknowledging that a defeat suffered should not have the power to destroy what was dear and precious to me.

109. Through general acceptance, science is the basis of the fields of knowledge that orient the roads towards discoveries required by the societal structure and the cultural tradition. Any scientific discovery is based on unalterable laws, motion, content, and purpose, which are the essence of studying realities through observation and experiment. From archaic times, humankind has benefited from all the discoveries that have brought progress and civilization, and that have contributed to the elimination of superstitions in the critical realms of existence. Science has brought undeniable benefits to all areas that have needed improvements in human conditions, and that have broadened the growth of research into new problems. Most scientists have devoted their efforts and intense intellectual activity to exploring, understanding, and experiencing the physical and natural world for the betterment of living conditions. Their successes were rewarded by the beneficial results obtained and were not expected as personal merits. However, there is a

category of scientists who have devoted their time and efforts to finding means of extermination commanded by the cruelty of the ruling powers of groups and nations seeking domination. Those scientists proved to have no different consciousness from those who hired them and rewarded them for killing people and for the consequences that followed. Such scientists represent a symbol of shame and offense for their thinking ability, contempt and disregard for their colleagues, and frightening threat to humanity.

110. We look for quality everywhere and in anything, whether natural or manufactured. The market is flooded with products, which must meet a quality standard in order to remain in competition, and that buyers appreciate by comparison with other products of the same kind. The quality of life depends on the general individual and social well-being and is measured by indicators considered standard for the entire population. However, the measurement of these indicators is not conclusive because they represent the level of wealth and employment between different

social strata, monetary compensation, education, and the degree of qualification to which the built environment refers. In addition, the quality of life is determined by the constitution of the character and by social relationships, which are complimented in a form compatible with understanding and accepting each other's attitude, behavior, and feelings. Moral qualities become indispensable in family relationships, in establishing a friendship, and in associating between partners engaged together in the same activity. Everyone has a different degree of evaluation of personal qualities and knows the extent to which those qualities can be revealed to others, just as everyone has a different level of appreciation of the distinctive attributes observed in others. The level of a harmonious communication comes from similar natures that are reflected in any relationship based on trust, appreciation, and mutual respect, and which enhance the values of life.

111. It is said that people are born with talents and are able to produce unimaginable beauties with special merits. If so, the world would not be gray and the existence would not smell of candle

wax. The world would be pink and the existence would smell like a rose. People who were born with special talents were rare, at intervals of tens and hundreds of years and perhaps at intervals of millennia. They were the ones who produced miracles in the fields of art, science, philosophy, and understanding some of the mysteries of life. They were the ones who guided the mind and soul toward a unique acknowledgment, and contributed to the enrichment of the human values. In general, people have no special talents, but some have the ability to develop skills through learning and by finding motivations to practice them easily as opposed to others who have to make efforts to learn and use them. The ability to discover expectations in the development of skills is determined by the recognition of special qualities and by personal confidence in the power to evaluate them for worthy purposes. The attention paid to the cultivation of skills leads to outstanding results that can be likened to those of an innate talent. People who are born with special talents are indeed rare, but those who learn to develop their abilities for valuable purposes deserve the same respect and admiration.

112. Some people have a strong body and demonstrate a stupendous power. Some others have a strong mind and prove a tremendous intelligence. Now and then, someone has them both, but that must be one of nature's rare mistakes. Society has power also, which is based on laws and regulations that have to be obeyed by everyone. A strong body is impressive especially when athletes display it in a sportive arena, but when physical power is exercised for abusing the weak, it should be considered an excess in committing a crime and should be punished as such. On the other hand, the power of the mind is guided by reason and the ability to analyze difficult situations in which conflicts are resolved through peaceful solutions and by establishing favorable conditions based on logic arguments. The power of intelligence determines the formation of a disciplined character and eliminates the influence of prejudices that could damage relationships with others as well as they might cause errors in reaching the right decisions. People with powerful intelligence channel their

thinking, feelings, and actions based on moral values, avoid influences that might compromise their choices, and are truthful to de commitments they make. The power of intelligence activates the resolution to accumulate those distinctive qualities on which the discipline of the mind is based and is joined by a strong confidence in the right judgment that could not be questioned.

113. Imitating someone is good as long as one's personality is not substituted with a false one. You like someone's behavior, the way that person talks, smiles, moves, and you want to have the ability to behave similarly. Do you know yourself well enough, don't you like the way you are, and would you like to be different? Perhaps someone else's way doesn't even match your personality. Perhaps imitating the behavior of a person you like is a forgery and a big mistake instead of a boon. It would be much better to try to get to know yourself, to carefully analyze your qualities and mistakes, to observe what would suit you best, and to change where you think a change would be appropriate and beneficial. What is worthwhile is to learn from others the

development of skills and knowledge that allow the absorption of new elements efficiently, and that allow an improvement of communication through interaction in social and individual exchanges. People who have produced human values at high levels have opened new avenues for research and become outstanding examples in the search for new perspectives and knowledge. Following their way of thinking is commendable especially if the cognitive process is enriched and brings new incentives in the potential for learning and knowledge.

114. The experts in linguistics say, and I quote the United Nations count *"Of the approximately 3,000 languages spoken in the world today, only some 78 have a literature. Of those 78, a scant five or six enjoy a truly international audience."* One can deduce from these figures the degree of education and culture that exists today worldwide. The languages of the peoples evolved in the rhythm of the development of civilizations and in relation to the societal systems that gave more or less importance to the use of language in the mode of communication. An evolved language is flexible and rich

in expressions, compared to a language from a low level of education that is rigid, poor in vocabulary, and difficult in expression. The beauty of a language does not necessarily consist in the sounds of words, but in the way of expressing ideas that denotes richness and flexibility and at the same time simplicity in phrasing. Today's science and technology introduce new words and expressions that influence the culture and way of communication that everyone must understand. The mode of thinking is also dictated by the language in which we express ourselves and which intertwines the relations of communication and exchange of information with our fellow citizens as well as with those who have a different nationality. Each language expresses a unique vision of the world, represents the human intellectual achievement, and deserves a same respect.

115. People like flowers for their beauty, color, and fragrance, just as they like plants for their foliage variety. They plant them, grow them, take care of them, and form ornamental gardens. Of all, I am most attracted to the cactus plant, which has no beauty, no bright color, and no fragrance,

rarely bears few flowers, but symbolizes the unparalleled power of survival. All species of cactus can survive for many years between rains or storms, living only with the previously stored water. The cactus appears and grows in the desert where the temperatures are usually unbearable for other plants, and where the lack of water for a long time would prevent the growth of natural vegetation. The spines that cover the plant form a protective blockade against predators as well as against the intense heat of the desert. Similar to the special constitution of the cactus, there are people with unusual survival power, able to overcome the greatest difficulties, with remarkable resources of self-defense, and with an exceptional will to overcome all obstacles that prevent a significant existence. Such people molded their strong personality through unusual efforts, are exemplary characters, and deserve the highest admiration.

116. Education is the measure of understanding. Knowledge of reality and the world is a vital necessity and a critical factor in the ability to survive the conditions in which the contemporary

societal development is continuously asserted. The circumstances that people face on a daily basis are complicated, interrelated, and require decisions in which those involved have an obligation to solve problems in such a way that the results obtained are clear and useful. Understanding and deciphering relationships between people reduces the friction that can occur at any time and that can aggravate an imminent danger. Education determines the level of understanding of the situations that occur daily, and influences the right choice of solutions by critically analyzing the determining cause and the effect that followed. The higher the education, the higher becomes the reasoning capacity. The logical way develops in relation to the information that the thought processes and offers a clear vision in the formulation of the opinions and the adoption of the correct decisions. People without the least basic education become parasites, dependent on others, a burden on society, and a constant threat to societal order and prosperity. Education brings the freedom to abandon the humiliating state of ignorance and inferiority. Ensuring a rudimentary education is crucial in eliminating the discrepancy between social classes, decreases animosity among people, and is critical in maintaining the material and cultural progress of society.

117. Until the twentieth century, there were very few women who affirmed themselves on the cultural, scientific, or political scene. They were considered unusual and exceptional trespassers into the exclusive domains of man. During the last decades of the twentieth century, man opened some of his doors to woman, neither because he wanted her to be as smart as he was, nor because he changed his ancestral opinion about her abilities, but because he needed her in the scrambled world he had designed, which is now ready to collapse. He is overwhelmed by struggles and fights with his fellow men as never before; he is confused by too many problems without solutions; he is unable to provide alone the supplies for himself and his family; and he is unable to find his proper pace in order to progress and to stand alone. No one is the master of the other, and except for physical strength, no one is superior or inferior to the other. They

are associated, as to be partners in this life, and they are dissimilar, as to become more complex identities through their achievements. Both of them are created to go side by side, to grow and evolve in a single world of equally constructed and shared values.

118. My oldest ancestor that I would like to think of was "Homo Habilis", who sat on the ground and carved a stone or a piece of wood to use in searching for his food. I'm sitting in my chair and type on the computer keyboard in search for information. Between him and me, there is a time span of about two millions years. Unfortunately, he was extinct from the human genus because his brain did not adapt and evolve to his environment. This means that I didn't inherit his genes and I'm glad for that because my brain does adapt and evolves just fine. We all come from a better design called "Homo Sapiens" who the experts say, could think. The superiority of the human species over the others resides in the power of thinking, language, and skill of organization. The human intelligence is magnificent when it comes to elaborate complicated projects to serve the human

life and the understanding of realities, to improve behavior, to keep unaltered the human values, and to initiate perspectives to be followed with greatness by the future generations. Humanity is the highest virtue and it is associated with the basic ethics of moral elevation, enlightened by the human intellect.

119. Reason and emotion are two traits that do not compliment each other. Reason is based on empirical and logical evidence and is expressed through thinking; emotion is triggered by external or internal stimuli and is expressed through subjective feelings. If they meet on the same road, one of them must give way to the other. The occurrence of daily problems requires understanding and discernment, and further, the evaluation of the probabilities of execution based on logic, and even further, the consideration of the factors that determine the possibilities of realization. It is a rigorous process of applying reasoning that does not admit confusing interpretations or approximations based on intuitive impressions. The choice of correct solutions for the considered problems is based on the logic applied, and does not

depend on the substratum of sensations and emotions. The reasoning ability is involved in daily situations in which the correct evaluation of the included factors is the basis for finding an acceptable result and in continuation for the application of the correct decisions. The ability to think rationally belongs to those who analyze information, trust the facts that are experienced, and eliminate argumentative opinions. The logical way of thinking is based on the organized mental process and on the controlled discipline of emotions that must be avoided in choosing critical decisions. Without any doubt, capacity to reason is the highest endowment a human being can have.

120. Everyone's personality is accentuated by the loyalty with which one serves the code of ethics that is self-imposed and is practiced. Honesty, trust, responsibility, are moral values learned and adopted throughout life, and which guide the formation of a stable character. Ethics has emerged since ancient times and has gradually developed as a major necessity in the application to life of individual moral values as well as in the constraint

of human behavior on the societal level. The simplest definition of ethics is the understanding and differentiation between good and evil, or more precisely, knowledge in the exertion of a right or wrong attitude. The right or wrong behavior is learned from experience and is adopted according to the appreciation of the moral values characteristic of each individual. The implementation over time of ethical principles forms a mode of conduct supported by a code of ethics that each individual builds and applies in daily life. Society cannot rely on the flexibility of the individual code of ethics and consequently establishes an ethical system based on moral values that is mandatory for the protection of the entire community. When a criminal is punished, the evaluation of the act committed is often questionable, but the code of ethics intervenes and the moral justification prevails. The knowledge, adoption, and practice of the individual and societal code of ethics represent the support of common existence and the security of a stable development.

121. Life is a journey of drops and dots, and each step is a purpose to make one forward

and remembering the one behind. We must learn, understand, think, and analyze our feelings every single step on the way. The societal conjunctures make us running toward gigantic purposes that are barely understood, and only exhaust our energies and our strength. Nevertheless, everything we intend to do has a purpose whether we plan it, or simply, it follows an insignificant act that we are unaware of. The goal we set out to achieve invigorates our mental faculties and brings our efforts into the desired state of use, in a coordinated system in which the desire for fulfillment prevails over doubts. Our skills are activated and progressively directed towards the process of a successful completion of the project designated for a certain purpose. A reason for a good cause is the best direction toward a motivated commitment, arouses the correct choices, incites the best in our behavior, and gives us the reward, which we deserve and never expected. People should find their meaning in life, understand it, work to achieve it with success, and leave on the side everything which is done just for the passing of time. First of all, they should define a purpose to know themselves, find who they really are, and spare no effort in becoming better with every choice and decision they make.

122. Knowledge is the power of intelligence to distinguish between good and evil, to take correct decisions, and to make right choices. We accumulate knowledge throughout life, from experiences, from studies, from educational institutions, and from relationships with people. There have been famous personalities in history, with an exceptional level of intelligence, who have made amazing contributions to the world of intellectual values. Those notabilities wanted to know everything that exists in the universe, in the physical and moral world, but they reached limits that they could not overcome. The inability to increase the capacity for knowledge beyond the possible limits they experienced, turned into frustration and most of them said that in reality their knowledge is nothing but null and void and in fact the knowledge they accumulated during life was non-existent. Of course, it was an unfair statement they made to themselves and it came from the fact that they failed to know everything they wanted to know.

There is no one who can call himself "omniscient" since reality is infinite and the ability to think is limited. Knowledge is required to be in continuous growth, and comes especially from the reasoning applied to the evidence demonstrated by the senses that provide details about the knowable reality and which is affirmed through a process of non-contradiction. Accumulating a vast knowledge of the world and life, generates personality, self-understanding, increases thinking ability, and balances the strengths and weaknesses of character.

123. People are trustworthy when they are interested in being like that, and when they think something good could come out for them. Honesty is very flexible and depends on how little or how much it is understood. Being honest means more than not lying, and an approximate definition of sincerity includes positive traits that include ethical and moral integrity, respect for fairness, and the adoption of honorable behavior. People who prove honesty are considered to be brave because they take responsibility for the attitude they show and which supports the depth of their feelings and

the correctness of their thinking. At the same time, there are people who make a lot of clamor about honesty, beat the drum loudly and noisily, saying that they do not want to have relationships with those who are dishonest, but when they are shown that they have made a mistake, or their behavior is not more appropriately, they get upset. People like to hear only what suits them and do not accept observations that touch their ego. How do we learn to fit a correct attitude when we do not accept the traits of an oscillating character or when the mistakes we observe urge us to intervene with observations? Only by gradual probing and experience. If sincerity is uncontrolled, it can become brutal and can hurt the feelings of those to whom it is addressed. There is a line that separates sincerity without danger of offense, from one that can be harmful and that can be followed by great regrets. The only aspect of honesty that admits any gradation from the lowest aspect to the highest consideration, is only for oneself, it is personal, and it is known to no one else.

124. "Generosity" is a big word for a small definition: helping the one in need. It is very easy for someone who has material wealth to be charitable and to make a contribution to those who need help. It is even an aspect of revitalization when the act of generosity is compensated by some amount of the reimbursement of taxes paid to society, and the one who has been so charitable does not feel much of the budget loss. Moreover, in the case of the very rich, the trumpeting in front of the media about the act of generosity brings advertising, increasing prestige and vanity, and admiration of the population. Generosity must be a discreet act and a form of personal virtue that is not required to be displayed or rewarded. To be charitable means to give material or spiritual help by understanding the needs of others, and finding a means of rapprochement that does not produce offense or humiliation. The appreciation of an act of generosity on the part of the recipient must be silenced because for someone who is honest, it is not important to mention it as a reason for reward. The generosity expressed to someone who needs moral support, time to analyze problems, or friendly advice that helps

maintain material stability, is the most precious gift that one can give and that brings the greatest self-satisfaction.

125. It is a delightful pleasure to watch the blooming vegetation with all the colors of flowers and leaves. The natural color green has the most numerous shades, in fact, that only botanists can count them. Similarly, there are human emotions that unfold on a large scale and are expressed in different shades, from the most delicate modulation to passionate outbursts. We call them love, hatred, anger, revenge, and so on. Especially the emotions felt for oneself are often confused and require a broader analysis to determine exactly the intensity that is activated. All emotions, each with its countless nuances, can be compared to a book that has many chapters, and each chapter is composed of paragraphs, phrases, words, letters, and punctuation. Why do we have so many emotions that are graded on such a large scale with so many and so varied shades? Scientists, philosophers, and experts in mental balance problems have studied this riddle for a long time, without finding a satisfactory answer to solve this mystery.

The results sought by experiments and assumptions confirmed only vague evidence that opened new avenues to try different theories. There is no precise answer, but it is universally known that the human mind is a miraculous system that does not admit to being known. The structure and vastness of the Universe is less difficult to understand than the human mind.

126. Moral weakness is a deviation from the normal functional state of one's individuality and is due to the lack of knowledge about the mental strength. Anyone born in a dysfunctional family ends up as an adult with a weak personality. Due to an undesirable climate in which abuses, violence, mistreatment prevailed, the strength of the mind which everyone possess, became concealed and prevented from functioning. Many of these individuals withdraw in shyness and disconnect from any social relationships, preferring to hide the weakness they suffer from and not make it recognized. Most weak people, however, denote irresponsibility, disregard any moral value, lie, steal, take revenge, terrorize those who cannot

defend themselves, and ridicule the power of the authorities. Only in these ways they can cover their weakness. Usually such individuals associate in groups that roam the streets, attack people, destroy property, commit arsons, and vandalize everything that is a source of income for them. Such antisocial elements are recruited as mercenaries by anyone who needs to carry out acts of blackmail, personal revenge or against a political organization, murder, terrorism, and any evil act that can be bought. Now and then, some of such people recover from their moral deviation by recognizing their infirmity and by working hard to overcome it through opening up and willingness to change.

127. The work for existence is not mandatory by law, but only by the necessity of providing a support for material and spiritual needs. People have to work to be able to live. The need for food, shelter, and the security of the essentials for survival are goals for which humankind has struggled and spared no effort to consolidate them since the beginnings of the first human settlements. Working in collective or individually brings not only

material benefit but also the satisfaction of achievements for new purposes that influence behavior and open paths of knowledge and understanding in the direction of dignity, discipline, and determination. There are people who do not need to work for their existence and the way they spend their time depends on everyone's choices. Many of them are on the road to moral decline, characterized by excessive indulgence in pleasure and luxury. There are also people who refuse to work and prefer to make a living by fraudulent means. Without finding an objective that justifies the physical or mental faculties, they are on the road to deterioration by losing vitality and the will to fit into a normal state. In conclusion, the need to work physically or intellectually, or both, is necessary to ensure an honorable existence and to maintain active the mental faculties in balance with the development of moral, cultural, and educational factors.

128. Music is the food of the soul and the most accessible and easiest to assimilate expression of cultural values. The harmony of sounds that brings calm, joy and pleasure to the human spirit is

mostly the wonderful work of composers of the past. It was the work of rhythm and equilibrium of the human soul itself that expressed the vision of feelings reflected in moments of pleasure or suffering. Of the many genres that exist today, at least one is favored by someone who feels the need to listen to it. The preferences are diverse and depend on the environment in which each one grew up, and also depend upon the influence of a certain gender that can favor the mood, thoughts and feelings, better than the others. In moments of loneliness and sadness, the harmony of classical music usually brings comfort, peace, and releases the anxiety of the mind giving it the vision of a satisfaction much sought. There is nothing more beneficent than a concert or an opera aria, or an enchanting song of country music, or a melancholic song of the blues music, which can soothe the most troubled thoughts and even make them disappear. Nevertheless, the youth in our days, prefers a kind of music in which harmony is totally lacking, which produces exaltation, and which is only an agglomeration of noises, combined with metallic instruments, and accompanied by vocal screams. This kind of so-called

„music" usually cannot be listened with much effect when the individual is alone, it is mostly addressed to crowds that become delirious, and it is extremely harmful. Considering the modern age as extremely complicated and hectic, perhaps, in this sense, this so-called „music" is useful in chronicling our current time.

129. It seems that the woman must be a very special creature since she can let out a bit of every spice to life. We don't know that for sure, but what is known is that she has a particular disposition, which if triggered by the right stimulus, can generate a remarkable willpower that is capable to exceed the highest expectations. Her personality is like a compound eye of an arthropod with innumerable facets that can move swiftly from one decision to another without any dilemma. Her feelings are deep from the least perceptible to the highest point of torrential passions. She is strong-minded, she loves, hates, protects, and destroys; she can be trustworthy, dedicated to a cause, ready to sacrifice herself, and kill in a blink of an eye for someone she loves; she is manipulative, revengeful, seldom

forgives, and uses chicanery to get what she wants. History gives many examples of women who built or destroyed empires just by whispering the right words in the ears of the men who had the power but fell under their charms. If she has beautiful traits, she knows the power of using them to subjugate someone she loves, or to ruin someone she hates. If she wants to hide her true feelings, the resource of her emotional state meant to deceive is always there, carefully crafted and in big supply. Whoever notices and tries to understand the vague smile on her face and the mystical light in her eyes, better be prepared for the unpredictable.

130. You and I have come a long way together. I revealed my thoughts and feelings to you with sincerity and good faith. If you got this far, I interpret that you paid attention to them and maybe you accepted their meanings just the way I expressed them even if some might have seemed disputable to you. During this long journey, I wished you to be close to my reasoning and I hoped that to some extent my opinions would be a reflection of the ones that you think similarly. I also hoped that something, no matter how

little from my writing would prove one day to be a worthwhile use of your time. After such a long time going together, now we have to take leave of one another. Maybe, eventually, now and then, you will remember my viewpoint regarding the human nature that I shared with you, my Reader, in this book. I shall always value the time we spent together, when I felt like talking to you, as a friend.

Printed in the United States
By Bookmasters